PROHIBITION NEW YORK CITY

SPEAKEASY QUEEN TEXAS GUINAN, BLIND PIGS, DRAG BALLS & MORE

DAVID ROSEN

Published by The History Press
Charleston, SC
www.historypress.com

First published 2020

Manufactured in the United States

ISBN 9781467146418

Library of Congress Control Number: 2020941792

Notice: The information in this book is true and complete to the best of our knowledge. It is offered without guarantee on the part of the author or The History Press. The author and The History Press disclaim all liability in connection with the use of this book.

For Jessica and Isabela and Dara and Zachary,
in the hope that the 2020s will be even more fulfilling than the 1920s.

Better a square foot of New York than all the rest of the world in a lump—
better a lamppost on Broadway than the brightest star in the sky.[1]

—Texas Guinan

CONTENTS

PREFACE

I've long been fascinated by periods of social disruption and how they help refashion American society. I came of age during the tumultuous 1960s and was part of the radical struggles that challenged—and changed—U.S. political policy and social life. It was a period of contestation, a transformative historical era. We may be on the verge of a comparable moment today.

Prohibition New York steps back a century from today to illuminate a remarkable different moment of Gotham's social dislocation—life during the Roaring Twenties. It continues the investigations I began with *Sex Scandal America: Politics, Morality & the Ritual of Public Shaming* (2009) and followed with *Sex, Sin & Subversion: How What Was Taboo in 1950s New York's Became America's New Normal* (2016).

This book is neither a biography of Texas Guinan nor a history of Prohibition in New York.[2] Rather, it uses her story as a keyhole into some of the secrets of Prohibition-era city life. Guinan (1884–1933) was a Broadway showgirl and early silent film star who, by chance, ended up running some of the city's grandest speakeasies. Her life illuminates a unique moment of social disruption in Gotham and throughout the nation. Without appreciating the illicit underworld that Texas symbolized, one can't fully grasp the roar of 1920s New York.

Texas, her speakeasies, the gangsters who backed her and the innumerable customers who patronized her clubs—whom she affectionately referred to as "suckers"—contested conservative moral authority. They, along with millions

Texas Guinan, 1920. *Wikimedia Commons.*

of Americans who went to local speaks throughout the country, challenged the power of the federal government—and conservative Christian forces—that imposed abstinence as the law of the land. These activists voiced the inebriated pleasures of drinking, nightlife socializing, jazz, interracial mixing, dancing, gay cruising, gambling and illegal drugs as well as what might happen later in the evening, including engagements at rent parties or sex circuses, encounters at drag balls, hookups with hookers and rendezvous at bathhouses. Collectively, they contributed to the repeal of Prohibition.

Prohibition went into effect on January 17, 1920, and was repealed on December 5, 1933, one month after Guinan died on a road trip in Vancouver on November 5, 1933. However, four years after the repeal of Prohibition, the federal government imposed prohibitions against the distribution, sale and consumption of marijuana. Federal authorities classified marijuana as a Title 1 drug, and this classification is still in place, although millions of Americans violate the existing laws and an increasing number of states across country have legalized marijuana for medical and recreational uses.

A century ago, Woodrow Wilson vetoed the National Prohibition Act, but a conservative Congress quickly overrode his veto and imposed abstinence for the next thirteen years. With Donald Trump as president and the 2020 election approaching, one can only wonder if a new era of Prohibition might be in store for America.

I would like to extend my personal thanks to a group of friends who helped me with this labor of love: Madeline Belkin, Chris Carlsson, Peter Hamilton, Inge King, Laura May, Linda Mochler, Donald Nicholson-Smith, Randolph Reynolds, Lianne Richie, John Galbreath Simmons and John Trinkl. And a special thanks to Inge for her patience educating me about picture editing and Lianne for her computer knowhow.

Finally, I would like to thank The History Press—and especially Banks Smither—for their support publishing this book, a work long in gestation.

Introduction

THE LURE OF TRANSGRESSION

What Is Acceptable?

January 15, 1920, was a cold night in Gotham, just six degrees Fahrenheit, but New Yorkers gathered in nightclubs, saloons, bars and local watering holes throughout the city to engage in an old-fashion wake, to enjoy one last drink and, collectively, bemoan the coming imposition of Prohibition. And drink they did.

They gathered on the Lower East Side at Max's Little Hungary on Houston Street and in midtown at Maxim's de Paris at Madison and 61st Street. In the heart of Times Square, they mingled at the Majestic, the Café de Paris, Jack's on 6th Avenue, Joel's at West 41st Street and 6th Avenue and at Lambs on 42nd Street.[3]

At Rector's, a legendary lobster palace located at Broadway and 44th Street, five hundred mourners raised their glasses in rousing revelry. At the throng's center stood Gilda Gray, the Ziegfeld Follies dancer famous for her scandalous shimmy. Tonight she was costumed as a handmaiden to Bacchus, the Roman version of Dionysus, the god of the grape harvest and joyous intoxication. The scantily clad Gray, poised before an effigy of the god, led a parade line through the assembled crowd. The guests, pushing and shoving, tore at the deity until little was left and its remains were finally placed in a coffin and taken from the room.[4] New York and the nation would never be the same.

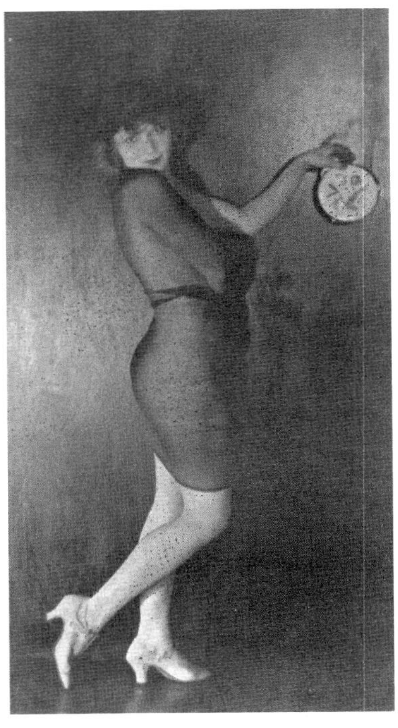

Gilda Gray. *Wikimedia Commons.*

People have been drinking alcohol in Gotham since before the city was settled. An apocryphal story from old claims that Henry Hudson served gin to a party of Lenape Indians in 1608 on what is today's Manhattan Island. According to this legend, "the Indians passed out, to a man." The often-forgotten part of the story is that the Lenape named the place Manahachtanienk—"the island where we all became intoxicated."[5]

Beer, cider, gin, rum and other intoxicating beverages were not only safer in early America, an era without potable water, but far more pleasurable than water or nonfermented fruit drinks. Benjamin Rush, a signatory of the Declaration of Independence and a representative to the Continental Congress, was one of the nation's leading early physicians. He believed that excessive alcohol consumption negatively affected both physical and psychological well-being. His belief was a truism of American medicine for two centuries, profoundly influencing moral beliefs and legitimizing the temperance movement.

For many conservative Americans, especially religious and secular moralists, drinking an intoxicating beverage was seen as a form of theft, the cost of each drink stealing valuable dollars from the family's pay-package. In a traditional patriarchal world, men made the income and controlled the family's purse strings; women were dependent on their husbands for money and were expected to meet all of the family's domestic obligations. Under conditions of financial stress, alcohol fueled domestic tensions, leading to violence, most often the husband abusing the wife or the father beating the child.

Today, what was once unacceptable has been mainstreamed. In the United States, alcohol is a $254 billion industry, and marijuana for medical purposes is legal in thirty-three states and for recreational purposes in fourteen states. Such is the legacy of Prohibition.[6]

PROHIBITION

World War I began in Europe in 1914, and the United States formally declared war on April 6, 1917. In April 1917, Gotham adopted a 1:00 a.m. closing time for bars. In December 1917, President Woodrow Wilson restricted beer brewing to 2.75 percent alcohol by volume (ABV) and imposed so-called temporary wartime prohibition that took effect in November 1918.[7] On December 18, members of Congress proposed the Eighteenth Amendment calling for national abstinence; in January 1919, Prohibition was ratified by forty-six states. The National Prohibition Act—popularly known as the Volstead Act after Representative Andrew Volstead (R-MN)—was implemented on January 16, 1919.

Prohibition grew out of a century-long campaign to contain the forces that were perceived as threats to the nation's moral order. Traditionalists railed against vice in every form, be it alcohol consumption, gambling, prostitution, birth control or obscenity in the arts. The Young Men's Christian Association (YMCA), the Woman's Christian Temperance Union (WCTU) and the Ku Klux Klan (KKK), among others, championed this movement.[8] The Prohibition Party was founded in 1869 and was the first political party to accept women as party members; the men-only Anti-Saloon League (ASL) was established in 1898. Anti-immigration proponents assailed Germans, Irish, Catholics and Jews as un-American for drinking alcoholic beverages.

The temperance campaign gained legitimacy during World War I and in the wake of the 1918 influenza epidemic in which an estimated 650,000 Americans died, including 30,000 New Yorkers.[9] The campaign culminated in not only the adoption of the Eighteenth Amendment but also the Nineteenth Amendment giving women the vote. It was a tumultuous era, one marked by social disruption that included a wave of strikes, political bombings and what became known as the first Red Scare. It included the Palmer Raids and the deportation of nearly 300 "aliens," including anarchists Emma Goldman and Alexander Berkman.[10]

Temperance was furthered by the strength of the eugenics movement, especially among scholars and "progressives" like Margaret Sanger. Albert Wiggam, a psychologist and national spokesperson for the eugenics movement, declared in 1924, "The Eighteenth Amendment, if it really prohibits, is the most tremendous 'eugenics law' ever passed in the world's history, because it will profoundly influence the health, sanity, and stamina of generations yet unborn." The historian Philip Wilson noted, "Although some eugenists focused on the threat of alcoholism, the majority, particularly

Interior of a crowded bar moments before midnight, June 30, 1919, when wartime prohibition went into effect in New York City. *Library of Congress Prints & Photographs Online Catalog (PPOC), Control Number 99405168.*

during Prohibition, pointed repeatedly to the interconnections between alcoholism, prostitution, and another bad habit, crime."[11]

Prohibition was in force for thirteen years—1920 to 1933—and evolved through three overlapping phases. The first ran from 1920 to 1923, from the imposition of the Eighteenth Amendment until New York State repealed the Mullan-Gage Act, the state's concurrent legislation. The second phase was Prohibition's glory days and lasted from 1923 to 1928, with innumerable swank speaks, celebrity culture and the wide-scale flaunting of the temperance law. Raids on the night of June 28, 1928, launched the third phase of Prohibition, which lasted until it was repealed. Each phase was characterized by a distinct speakeasy scene, attendant popular culture, gangster activities and enforcement practices. Taken together, speakeasies defined New York nightlife during the Roaring Twenties—they were the place to be.

As Prohibition was slowly institutionalized, ever-resourceful New Yorkers adapted to the tougher conditions and refashioned the speakeasy scene. Compared to the saloons and grand lobster palace of the 1910s, the new nightlife environment required a different economics. Speaks had to be smaller and more affordable venues to both hide from vigilant enforcement officials and safeguard against the expenses incurred if the club was raided, inventory seized and the speak shut down.[12]

Prohibition's second phase was marked by the opening of Texas Guinan's first speak, the El Fey on West 45th Street, in 1924. It saw the opening of other legendary watering holes in Times Square area—dubbed "the wet zone"—like the Stork Club and the Silver Slipper, uptown in Harlem like the celebrated Cotton Club and Connie's Inn and in the Village at Club Gallant. These and many other speaks gave the Roaring Twenties its glamour, its magic—its roar.

However, given the period's precariousness, noted clubs like the Moulin Rouge, the Plantation and Palais Royal, home of the Paul Whiteman Orchestra, succumbed to bankruptcy. One unanticipated consequence of the institutionalization of Prohibition saw gangsters take control of city nightlife; not surprising, Texas's El Fey was run by Larry Fay and backed by Owney Madden, two legendary Gotham mobsters.

Lips That Touch Liquor Shall Not Touch Ours. Satirical photograph of teetotaler women, still from an 1890s movie, *Kansas Saloon Smashers*, filmed in Edison's Black Maria studio. *Wikimedia Commons.*

New York City deputy police commissioner John A. Leach (*right*) watching agents pour liquor into the sewer following a raid during the height of Prohibition. *Library of Congress Picture Resources, cph.3c23257.*

In 1926, as Prohibition enforcement floundered, the U.S. government began deliberately poisoning illegal liquor. As Deborah Blum, author of *The Poisoner's Handbook*, found, "By all accounts, that rather murderous government program—which involved adding toxic contaminants to the industrial alcohol being siphoned off by bootleggers—killed more than 10,000 people."[13]

Prohibition's final phase took its toll on city nightlife, with big spenders—Texas's favorite sucker—no longer spending as lavishly on good times. More troubling, as gangsters gained control of the liquor trade, they diversified into syndicates with stakes in allied industries including nightclubs, hotels, laundry services and other rackets like gambling, prostitution and the fledgling drug trade.

The Volstead Act was initially enforced through the Internal Revenue Bureau's (IRS) Prohibition Unit. However, due to the IRS's failure to halt the mounting alcohol trade, enforcement was reorganized and, in April 1927, the agency was transferred to the Department of the Treasury and rebranded the Bureau of Prohibition. As federal temperance policy continued to erode, the Prohibition Bureau was, in July 1930, again transferred, this time to the Department of Justice. Finally, after Franklin Roosevelt's election in 1932 but before repeal finally took effect, this wayward agency was shunted off to the Justice Department's Bureau of Investigation (later renamed the Federal Bureau of Investigation).

SPEAKEASY CITY

New York's five boroughs consolidated into Gotham in 1898, and by 1920, its population topped 5.6 million. Not only did it dwarf all other American cities, being double the size of Chicago, but it also claimed one million more residents than London. It had fulfilled Walter Benjamin's vision, on its way to becoming—after World War II—the capital of the twentieth century, superseding Paris, the capital of the nineteenth century, and anticipating the ascendancy of Shanghai, the likely capital of the twenty-first century.[14]

No one knows the true number of speakeasies that operated in Gotham during Prohibition. (Appendix 3 lists some known operations.) In 1925, it was estimated 100,000 illegal alcohol drinking nightclubs operated throughout the city, ranging from upscale speakeasies to middle-class bars and cabarets to working-class blind pigs. Some were distinguished as much by the wealth and social standing—or lack thereof—of their respective clientele as by the highest-quality illegal champagne, spirits, wines and beers they served. Others offered lowest-grade bathtub rot-gut hooch brewed in the speak's cellar. All sought to promote good times, however defined, for the upscale social set and even down-and-out bar flies. Prohibition saw the speak replace the once-popular saloon and nightclub; the gangster replaced the neighborhood barkeep as the boss of the goodtime scene. In this process, New York nightlife was reinvented.

During Prohibition, speakeasies were the place to be. They earned their legendary reputation as venues that facilitated the transgression of the socially acceptable. They were private clubs that served illegal alcohol and fostered a culture of sociability that could not be found in any other popular nightlife venue. They had peepholes, secret passwords and private keys, and some required a membership card with the necessary fake name and address and a sponsor to get in. Although, simply saying, "Joe sent me," was often

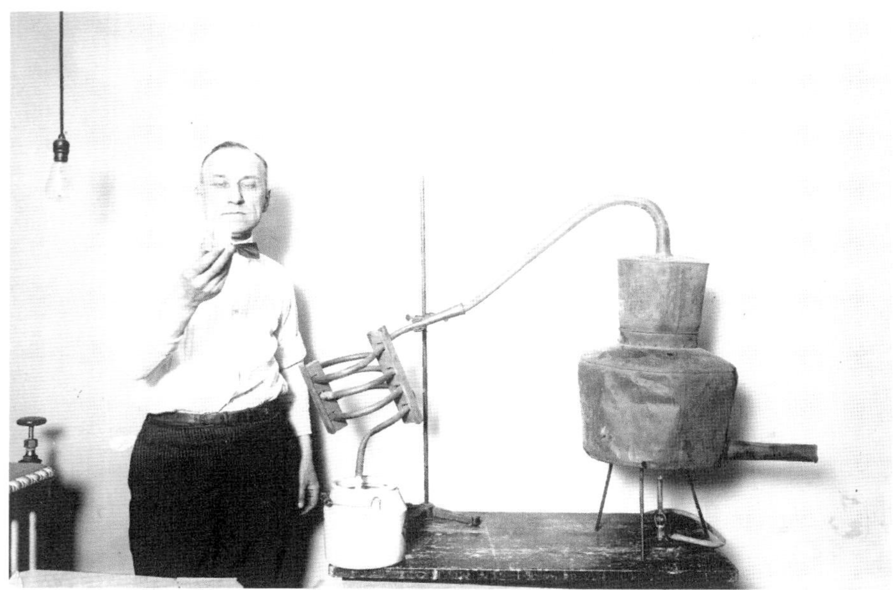

Moonshine still confiscated by the Internal Revenue Bureau photographed at the Treasury Department, *Digital ID cph 3b42140.*

good enough. Some offered dinner, music and dance, while others enabled patrons to rub shoulders with well-to-do social worthies and big-name celebrities as well as prostitutes, homosexuals and gangsters. Some sold ginger ale and soda at inflated prices, and then, surreptitiously, the barfly added a touch of alcohol to the drinks. As its very name suggests, one had to "speak easy" when ordering an intoxicating drink.

The term *speak-easy*, which was originally hyphenated, seems to derive from Irish miners working in western Pennsylvania. The great '20s editor and wit H.L. Mencken attributed the term to immigrants: "Spake asy, now, the police are at the dure." A late nineteenth-century journalist, Samuel Hudson, insisted that the term came from Pittsburgh miners before being popularized in Philadelphia and New York. A different version of the story was reported by the *New York Times* in 1890, identifying one Kate Hester, a McKeesport, Pennsylvania saloonkeeper, who, in 1888, allegedly quieted rowdy mine worker patrons with the injunction, "Speak easy, boys! Speak easy!"

The Oxford English Dictionary suggests that the term originated much earlier, in the 1690s, to designate a place where guests were invited to dine, drink wine and have a good time. By the mid-nineteenth century, a "softy shop" or "speak-house" referred to a room in a convent or ministry where guests were invited to converse and drink. Most insightfully, E.P. Sanford, chief of the research division, U.S. Department of Justice Bureau of Prohibition, defined a speak quite succinctly as "a table, two chairs, and a bottle of liquor." Formally, he elaborated that it was "a place where liquor is sold illegally more or less openly to the public by the drink or in bulk."

On January 16, 1920, Prohibition went into effect, making it illegal to manufacture, import, distribute and sell intoxicating beverages. Most importantly, the federal law did not make it illegal to produce alcohol for personal consumption or for medical and industrial purposes—legal loopholes that many took advantage of to enjoy illegal intoxicants.

Under the Volstead Act, some fifteen thousand doctors, veterinarians, pharmacists and dentists applied for permits to prescribe select quantities of alcohol to address a host of illnesses, from cancer to depression.[15] While visiting New York in 1932, Winston Churchill received a prescription for "the use of alcoholic spirits especially at mealtime. The quantity is naturally indefinite but the minimum requirements would be 250 cubic centimeters."[16] Speaks were venues of social transgression that contested the church for the nation's soul; they were venues in which virtue and sin battled—and sin won!

Speakeasies and the New Woman

"In the speak-easies mixed drinking of mixed drinks was the rule," noted one Prohibition-era wag, "the women bellying up to the bar with the men, skirt short, stockings rolled below the knee, and corsets sometimes checked at the cloak room."[17] Of all the transgression that took place at the speakeasy, the active presence of women most threatened the propriety and moral rectitude proclaimed by many American traditionalists. Not only was a "new woman" coming onto the historical stage, but she was an unprecedented sexualized one at that.

The new woman profoundly threatened traditional Christian patriarchal values. Throughout the nineteenth century, many American women were physically restrained by corsets and trailing skirts. In the decades after the Civil War, an increasing number of women were urbanized. They joined the workforce in ever-growing numbers and had money in their pockets. A growing number secured an education, some going to college and postgraduate study and even entering traditional male professions. This process escalated in the World War I era as men were called to military service.

Flapper drawing. Russell Patterson, *Where There's Smoke There's Fire*, 1930s. *Wikimedia Commons.*

Women deployed fashion to empower their bodies, transforming themselves from passive objects of representation to active subjects of performance. Clothes, as Angela Latham reminds us, are "a particularly potent way to display and play with notions of respectability, allure, independence, and status and to assert a distinctive identity and presence." The fashions of the first decades of the twentieth century symbolized and facilitated the emergence of a transformed, eroticized femininity. As Latham notes, "The fashionable flapper was correctly perceived to present a serious challenge to the tenacious influence of American Victorian traditions of feminine behavior and display."[18]

The biggest battle that took place over the development of the new woman's sexuality was fought over her face. For generations, a much made-up female face outside the theater signaled a prostitute—a "painted lady." By the 1880s, makeup had begun, as one historian noted, "to cross from the stage into everyday life." And by the turn of the twentieth century, cosmetics—and especially lipstick—symbolized a woman's new freedom.

Makeup captured the essence of an age in which "appearances were fluid and social rank unstable." As Kathy Peiss argues, makeup "assert[ed] worldliness against insularity and sexual desire against chastity." So powerful was its appeal that over the two decades between 1909 and 1929, cosmetics sales rose

Flapper. *Wikipedia Commons.*

tenfold. The traditionalist's battle against the "false face" was eroded as women, especially younger high school graduate working girls and college students, used makeup to "transform the spectacle of themselves into self-conscious performances."[19] By the time Prohibition arrived, the line between a painted lady and a respectable woman was a thing of the past.

If lipstick was important to the rituals of public display, it was also essential for the most intimate ritual of private engagement, kissing. The "petting question," as it was known during the first decades of the twentieth century, went through a fundamental revision by the time Prohibition arrived. Up until then, among college coeds, "nice girls" did not kiss until they were engaged. But by the '20s, "the polling of coeds showed that fairly indiscriminate petting was the rule."[20] Such indiscriminate petting was not uncommon at speakeasies.

Equally threatening, the new woman discarded the old-fashioned corset and lifted the dress's hemline, freeing her physical movement. This transformed her very step. And as the hemline rose and her skirt crept up above her knee, the ankle and calf became a theater of fleshy erotic display framed by shoes and suggestive stockings. She applied lipstick, bobbed her hair, smoked Sweet Corporals, visited a speakeasy, danced to jazz, drank "Bronx cocktails," flirted, knew about birth control and kissed her beau but rarely engaged in premarital intercourse. With the adoption of the Nineteenth Amendment in 1920, she gained the right to vote. The Roaring Twenties new woman was the flapper.

During the '20s, the speak was but one of an ever-growing number of arenas of public life that welcomed single women. Other spaces included movie theaters and dance clubs as well as beaches and amusement parks, all venues of public erotic display and encounter. Venues promoting the female performance artist included the fading burlesque shows, Broadway plays and revues and carnival "girl shows," all catering to male fantasy. The eroticized female was also the star visual attraction of the older postcard pornography and the newer movie industry. Male homosexuality found its most radical form of expression in the surprisingly popular and erotically provocative "drag balls" that took place in New York and other cities. Sexuality—especially when lubricated with alcohol—saturated the Prohibition era's secret social life. It infused the speakeasy with its most threatening, transgressive appeal—and New York was the nation's center of transgression.

At some Gotham speaks, eroticism was stimulated by mixing of differences—whether of people from different races, of different sexual orientations or (sometimes) of different classes. They were titillated by a festive informality and the presence of Tijuana bibles, risqué sex magazines often sold under the counter. Patrons were solicited for sexual engagement through the innumerable hookups between people from the same or the other gender or between a prostitute and her john. The atmosphere was one of intrigue. At the speak, as the historian George Chauncey observed, "If whites were intrigued by the 'primitivism' of black culture, heterosexuals were equally intrigued by the 'perversity' of gay culture."[21]

Speaks were where one went to break the law. They were the nexus of a peculiar historical conjunction: pleasure, perversion and inebriation. Having a drink at a speakeasy was an act of transgression: One was committing a crime. When one entered a speak, one crossed the line between the socially acceptable and the illegal and, for many, the immoral. By breaking the law, one transgressed from the world of regulated pleasure (in other words, traditional heterosexual Christian values) to an experience of pleasure that could be unregulated, unpredictable and uncontrollable. This quest for pleasure would define post–World War II consumer culture.

QUEEN OF THE SPEAKS

Texas Guinan was a legendary Roaring Twenties personality, the queen of Gotham's speakeasy life; one can get a small sense of her on surviving YouTube videos. (See Appendix 2.) She was, as someone said, "blonde and blowsy and could match any man in a fist fight."[22] She was "brassy" and a "broad," when those terms had a subversive significance, words that once condoned an adored but different kind of woman, a '20s new woman. Guinan fashioned what became known as café society out of her own dynamic, irrepressible persona. She is a keyhole into the great resistance that undermined and ultimately led to Prohibition's repeal. One often unappreciated fact, Texas reminded her audiences, "I have never touched a drop of liquor in my life. It doesn't appeal to me."[23]

Guinan's speaks welcomed Gotham's grand celebrities like Al Jolson; the Gershwins, George and Ira; and Mae West. Regulars included James "Gentleman Jimmy" Walker and writers Ring Lardner, Damon Runyon and Heywood Broun as well as members of the Algonquin Round Table writers gang. Actors Tom Mix and George Raft often visited, as did gossip columnists Walter Winchell, Ed Sullivan and Mark Hellinger. Future stars like Rudolph Valentino, Ruby Keeler and Barbara Stanwyck got their starts performing at one of her clubs. Well-heeled worthies like Reginald "Reggie" Vanderbilt, Harry Payne Whitney and Walter Chrysler came to have a good time. Texas was intimate with leading gangsters like Arnold Rothstein, Dutch Schultz and Owney Madden, who financed many of her speaks. Busted by Prohibition agents, Guinan was repeatedly acquitted by trial juries.

Tex's most celebrated club was the El Fey, which opened on May 1, 1924, at the height of Prohibition. A swastika was embossed on the front window. In the era before Hitler, Larry Fay, the club's founder, saw it as a good luck symbol. It served as the only indication that the club was a speak. Texas was, in the words of her manager, John Stein, "the greatest of the queens of merriment, of the courtesans, and of all the despots of hilarity of her time."[24] She greeted patrons with an oversized Stetson hat, shrill police whistle and a stream of invectives, most notably her legendary catchphrase, "Hello, sucker!" She didn't so much insult her guests as welcome them with a slap on the face—and they loved it.

An older Texas Guinan. *Billy Rose Theatre Division, New York Public Library Digital Collections.*

Tex was a woman of her age, forty years old when she became a speakeasy celebrity, a bigger-than-life personality who fronted New York's toughest gangsters and for whom, as Stein noted, "democracy became her slogan, good fellowship her only standard."[25] She was well known for applying perfume to her fingertips so that those who shook her hand had something to remember her by.

Characters based on her have appeared in numerous Hollywood movies, including *Night After Night*, a 1932 film starring Mae West modeling herself after Texas and costarring George Raft, a former Madden muscle who got his starting working for Texas. The '39 release *The Roaring Twenties* has a character based on Texas, Panama Smith, played by Gladys George. In '45, Betty Hutton plays Guinan in *Incendiary Blonde*, and in 1961, Phyllis Diller portrays her in *Splendor in the Grass*. Texas appears in Francis Ford Coppola's 1984 hit, *The Cotton Club*, as the character "Vera," played by Diane Lane. But few people really know this oh-so-'20s figure.

This book places the legendary Guinan in the social context of New York's rip-roaring '20s, at the center of the city's booming underworld scene of illegal drink, gambling, prostitution, jazz, race mixing, pansy parties and other illicit indulgences. It was, in Stein's words, "the greatest, maddest, most joyous, most tragic city in the world, the lights flared brighter, jazz flared louder than ever before."[26] Her clubs welcomed some of the city's swankest swells, movie stars, politicians, madams, writers, musicians, good-time partygoers and the toughest sharks. Texas lived in the Village, ran clubs in the midtown wet zone and was a regular at some Harlem Whites-only jazz joints. New York was her home, and she illuminates city life in a unique and revealing way.

However, Texas was not a part of some of Gotham's other social underworlds. While she rubbed shoulders with city swells and cultural lions, she was part of neither set. She lived in Greenwich Village but had little to do with either the young bohemians remaking avant-garde culture or the immigrant Italians and African Americans calling it home. She rarely traveled outside Manhattan, a foreigner to the city's rapidly growing ethnic and working-class communities where a different order of speakeasies flourished. She had little to do with the real African American scene flowering amid the Harlem Renaissance, seemingly never having attended a mixed-race speak, late-night rent party or sex circus; there are no reports of Black people attending her—apparently all White—clubs. Nor was she familiar with the gay clubs or popular drag balls. She did, however, volunteer for innumerable charity fundraisers.

Not surprising, a form of the speakeasy remains alive today as a venue of suggestive intrigue, of socially accepted lawbreaker. In New York, speaks are popular among the very hip as unlicensed party spots and underground, invitation-only hangouts. Few recall that "hipsters" originally meant someone who carried an alcohol-filled hipflask during Prohibition. Today's hideaways include, in New York's Lower East Side, the Violet Hour, the Back Room and PDT (aka Please Don't Tell) and, in Williamsburg, Rye. They are discreetly located on anonymous streets, often with no name or address on the door. The city's most famous surviving speak remains Chumley's at 86 Bedford Street in the Village. Founded in 1922 by socialist Leland Stanford Chumley, it was long home to such literary notables as Scott Fitzgerald, William Faulkner, John Steinbeck, Ernest Hemingway, Allen Ginsberg and Norman Mailer. It closed in 2013 for renovation and is now, once again, open for business.

Manager Stein reported that the girl from Texas once reflected wistfully on her life, "I would rather have a square inch of New York than all the rest of the world in a lump." This book, hopefully, will be her square inch.

1
PARTY TIME

Party Girl

In 1922, as Prohibition descended on New York, Emile Gervasini, impresario of the Beaux Arts Café, a cabaret on West 40th Street, invited Texas Guinian to attend the opening night party for his new speakeasy, the Gold Room. At one point during the festive evening, Guinan, a local theatrical and movie talent, was encouraged to take the stage. She mixed song with storytelling, and the patrons wouldn't let her stop! Entranced by her captivating presence, they forced Gervasini to keep his speakeasy open until 5:30 a.m., well after curfew. Gervasini was so impressed he offered Tex a job as the club's greeter. New York nightlife would never be the same.

Texas was then performing her cowgirl act at Broadway's Winter Garden Theatre. A real cowgirl from Texas who had costarred with William S. Hart in many early one- and two-reel westerns, Guinan came to New York more than a decade earlier to pursue a career on Broadway and found modest success. Big, brassy and a bottle blond, she played her cards in Gotham, Europe and Hollywood; at thirty-eight, just as Prohibition was being imposed, she was hitting her prime. A lifetime in entertainment led to a night that changed her life and the city's nightlife.

At the Gold Room, Texas furthered the role of the female onstage hostess, the master of ceremonies pioneered by Sophie Tucker. What is more, she created the floor show, a Broadway staple. While Tex was the host and main attraction, she added Joe Fejer, a Hungarian violinist, and the noted pianist and composer Sigmund Romberg to her show. As host, Tex received $100 a week, plus tips—$1,542 in 2020 dollars. "Shaking hands with her customers was about Texas' only method of allurement," recalled John Stein, her manager. "She began speaking to her guests as they entered," he added. "Texas never forgot a face or name and often some celebrity or millionaire would find himself blushing at an unexpected familiarity but she would shortly turn his uneasiness into a sort of thrill at the precocity."[27]

Tempted by a competing offer from Joe Pani, who ran the King Cole Room, she moved her show, with Joe Fejer and his combo, to the Knickerbocker Hotel. It was a smashing success. A lucrative counteroffer quickly followed from Gervasini, and she returned to the Gold Room. Texas was the city's hottest attraction.

The reopening of the Gold Room was a major social event. As an attendee recalled, the gala was "jammed with glitter and exotic fragrance." Among those in attendance were former president Woodrow Wilson's daughter Margaret; Dorothy Caruso, the wife of the legendary tenor; the celebrated

Rudolph Valentino and Natacha Rambova, 1923. *Wikimedia Commons.*

actor John Barrymore; and Mrs. Anne Harriman Vanderbilt, one of America's wealthiest women. Tex extended a special invitation to Rudolph Valentino, who earlier had worked for her as a flower boy when he first arrived in America and now was at the height of his fame. Valentino insisted that he would only attend with his second wife, Natacha Rambova, if Texas made sure that his first wife, Jean Acker, would not be present. Acker had a habit of greeting Rudi and Natacha "with a loud and pronounced hiss." Texas persuaded Acker not to attend.

Amid the opening night festivities, however, a strangely dressed woman accompanied the socialite Peggy Hopkins Joyce. The guest was "about the wildest looking woman that Texas had ever seen," a participant observed. She wore a garish red wig, a low-cut black velvet evening gown and a diamond necklace and earrings. Most striking, her makeup was glaringly drawn in red, white and blue.

Greeting Tex, Joyce introduced the mysterious guest as the Countess of Itch from Cuba. Texas immediately recognized her as none other than Acker and saw catastrophe in the making. She warned Valentino and then made an ingenious proposition. Stein, who attended, vividly recalled the scene:

> *Miss Guinan led Miss Acker out on the floor and introduced her as the Countess of Itch, the former wife of Rudolph Valentino. Mr. Valentino then came forward. "There is a gentleman who desires the honor of your partnership in the next dance, Countess," Texas said. "Let me present the Count of Scratch."*

To the song "The Girl I Left Behind Me," the couple began to dance.[28]

"Hello, Sucker!"

Texas Guinan fronted New York's most notorious speakeasy, the El Fey Club, located at 123 West 45th Street, as the second phase of Prohibition got underway. Nils "Thor" Granlund—long known as "NTG"—introduced Texas to rackets boss Larry Fay, who offered her an opportunity to host his new club, which had opened in 1922. Described as the "horse-faced racketeer," Fay was the boss of the taxicab racket and called "Sweetheart" by those who dared.[29] No one forgot that one of Fay's backers was Owney "the Murderer" Madden, one of the city's leading mobsters. The El Fey

Nils Thor Granlund, *Billboard* January 10, 1942. *Wikimedia Commons.*

had a peephole and required a membership card to get in. It featured silk-covered walls, food and drink, skimpily clad showgirls and a tiny dance floor "the size of a small white envelope." Popular entertainer Jimmy Durante found it "more like an intimate party." Texas became the El Fey's hostess on May 1, 1924.

Stanley Walker, an editor of the *New York Herald Tribune* and author of the Jazz Age classic *The Night Club Era*, knew Texas well. His observation gives a sense of this bigger-than-life speakeasy legend: "Texas Guinan, in her fashion, during the boom times of the twenties combined the curious and admirable traits of Queen Elizabeth, Machiavelli, Tex Rickard, P.T. Barnum and Ma Pettingill." (George "Tex" Rickard ran Madison Square Garden in the '20s and is credited with staging the first $1 million boxing match; Ma Pettingill is a character performed by Maude Eburne, who acted in dozens of films between 1930 and 1949, in *Ruggles of Red Gap* (1935), costarring Charles Laughton.) As Walker observed, "The secret of her success was her candor. She told people they were fools, and were being rooked, and they liked it....Turned loose in a night club she could perform wonders."[30] Sophie Tucker recalled that Texas "had something that made everybody feel instantly at ease and ready for a good time." Edmund Wilson had a cooler perception, finding her a "formidable woman, with her pearls, her prodigious gleaming bosom, her abundant and gleaming beautiful bleached yellow coiffure, her bear-trap shining white teeth."

Texas was celebrated for her legendary catchphrases such as "Don't give a sucker a break!" She made famous a host of other sayings that became part of the '20s lexicon. "Butter and egg men" referred to generous tippers, and "Give the little lady a great big hand" was asked of patrons in recognition of a showgirl's performance.[31] Other memorable cracks of hers were: "Remember he may be all the world to his mother, but he is just a cover charge to you"; "Never let a fool kiss you and never let a kiss fool you"; "Virtue pays—if you can find a market for it"; and "Home is a great place—after all the other places have closed." Her toughness is enshrined in the alleged comment of one of her regulars: "Reach down in your heart, Texas, and get me a piece of cracked ice."[32] (See Appendix 1 for some more of Texas's one-liners.)

Party Time Texas Style

The El Fey was formally incorporated as the El Fey Club and, according to Stein, "the first sophisticated organized rendezvous for selling liquor. It gave the public a taste of the brew which Mr. Volstead had put his curse upon and it also gave the public a peep over the transom into the glamour of the underworld."[33] Stein was an El Fey late-night regular and intimately familiar with its upscale culture. He described it as "a long smoke filled room festooned with bright colored hangings." The club was tightly packed with small tables and chairs and crowded with festive, inebriated patrons. Showgirls selling cigarettes and various trinkets slithered through the club in scanty outfits. Stein knew a cigarette girl, Ethel, whom he recalled as "a charming girl in blue satin trousers and wearing a crimson sash [who] comes offering cigarettes, arriving at each table like a blown wisp of silk or a moth to a flower." Another girl wandering among the tables was Kitty Cripps, "a smart girl in black with silver flowers on her hips," who offered large dolls that ever-gallant male customers bought for their female companions.

The dance floor was jammed with merry partygoers. Stein paints a clear picture of the festive atmosphere:

> *In a little open space, scarcely large enough for a dozen people to stand, twenty couples, with heads or ears or lips pressed tightly together, managed somehow to move in a cheek to cheek mockery of a dance.*
>
> *The dancing was so thick that collision was inevitable. One couple, bumped strongly in postern at an unstable moment, rolled deliciously on the floor. Their eyes looked upward with most humorous surprise and appeal but no anger. They were like government bonds, begging not to be walked upon.*
>
> *A jazz band blazed blatantly an unending rhythm. Waiters pushed their way through the throng, red faced and nervously trying to balance their trays of silver topped bottles and elaborately prepared sandwiches above the heads of the revelers.*

However, past midnight, a stir filled the club: the Queen had arrived. Stein captures the excitement of Texas's appearance:

> *Suddenly there crashed in a long, loud blast of sound from the basses; the pianist dug his slender fingers into the ivories; the leader's baton was held high and trembled like a Florida palm in a hurricane....*
>
> *"Ya—a-a-ay, Texas," bawled the crowd.*

> *She made her entrance, with all the night-owl energy of her roistering personality. She was gowned in clinging, flaming red. Her hair—burnished gold—tumbled, brushed and curled in riotous unconventionality.*
>
> *You knew she was close to forty, yet she looked rather ageless. She pranced in, her arms aloft, her crimsoned lips broadened in a brilliant smile—Why not? Look at the capacity business. And at her heels a dozen or so more semi-nude dancing girls, laughing, chattering, fluttering.*
>
> *"Hello! Sucker!," the Queen has shouted, then stood beaming, sparkling, effervescing.*[34]

Officially, New York nightlife formally ended at 1:00 a.m., and many speaks stayed open until 3:00 a.m. But the El Fey didn't close until 5:00 a.m., keeping the party going til dawn. While the club legally could hold only eighty patrons, it often jammed in two hundred or more people. Alcohol passed through a hole in a wall that connected the speak to a tenement building next door to keep liquor storage off the premises. Popular legend suggests that the El Fey offered watered-down scotch for $1.50 a drink and charged $25 for a bottle of ginger ale champagne. Rumor has it that Guinan and Fay took in more than $700,000 during one ten-month period; this would be equivalent to $10.5 million in 2020 dollars.[35]

The club featured a troupe of forty scantily clad fan dancers dubbed the "Guinan Graduates"; they performed at Texas's many other clubs. Ruby Keeler and George Raft got their starts at the club. Because of limited space, they often performed provocatively close to the customers. Most were young, between thirteen and sixteen; Keeler was fourteen when she joined the line. Keeler dated Johnny "Irish" Costello, a bootlegger. However, she fell in love with Al Jolson, and this caused a minor scandal, forcing her to flee New York for Hollywood and a movie career.[36] Others who got their start working for Texas were Lillian Roth and Stanwych as well as such lesser-known performers of the '20s as Irene Delroy, Claire Luce and Frances Upton. New York's mayor Grover Whalen (whom Walker replaced in 1926) denounced the Graduates as a little gang of prostitutes.[37]

In 1926, after the El Fey was closed down and the front door padlocked, Larry Fay drew a D on the club's sign, rechristening the joint the Del Fey, and started serving loyal patrons. The Prince of Wales (later King Edward VIII) visited New York and repeatedly came to the club to see what made speaks so popular. On one visit, he joined the fight promoter Tex Rickard and cowboys from the Ringling Brothers Circus.[38] The patrons cheered the prince as one of the fellas.

Left: Ruby Keeler, by Alfred Cheney Johnston, 1920s. *Wikimedia Commons.*

Right: Barbara Stanwyck, "Ziegfeld Girl," by Alfred Cheney Johnston, circa 1924. *Wikimedia Commons.*

Taking advantage of the padlocking of the El Fey, Tex, invoking the mocking spirit of the era, turned the episode into a stage production, *Padlocks of 1927*. The review opened at the Shubert Theatre with a smashing send-off. As reported in the fledgling *Time* magazine, "She [Guinan] makes her entrance riding down the aisle on a white Arabian horse." Holding his nose, the unnamed reviewer applauded it with faint praise:

> *It is not a revue at all. It is less clever, more loud, bawdy, vulgar and—to people who like that sort of thing—vastly more entertaining than a Times Square revue could ever be, for the revue is not native while the night club is—even in a theatre. It has the perfection of a weed that grows unashamedly where Nature intended.*[39]

The reviewer failed to acknowledge that the music was by Lee David, Jesse Greer and Henry Tobias; that the book was by Paul Smith and Ballard MacDonald; and that the lyrics were by the legendary Billy Rose. It had a cast of over forty performers, including Raft, A.S. "Pop" Byron and Helen Shipman, well-known actors in the 1920s and '30s. Tex sang two tunes by Rose and MacDonald, "If I Had a Lover" and "The Tap Tap." While the

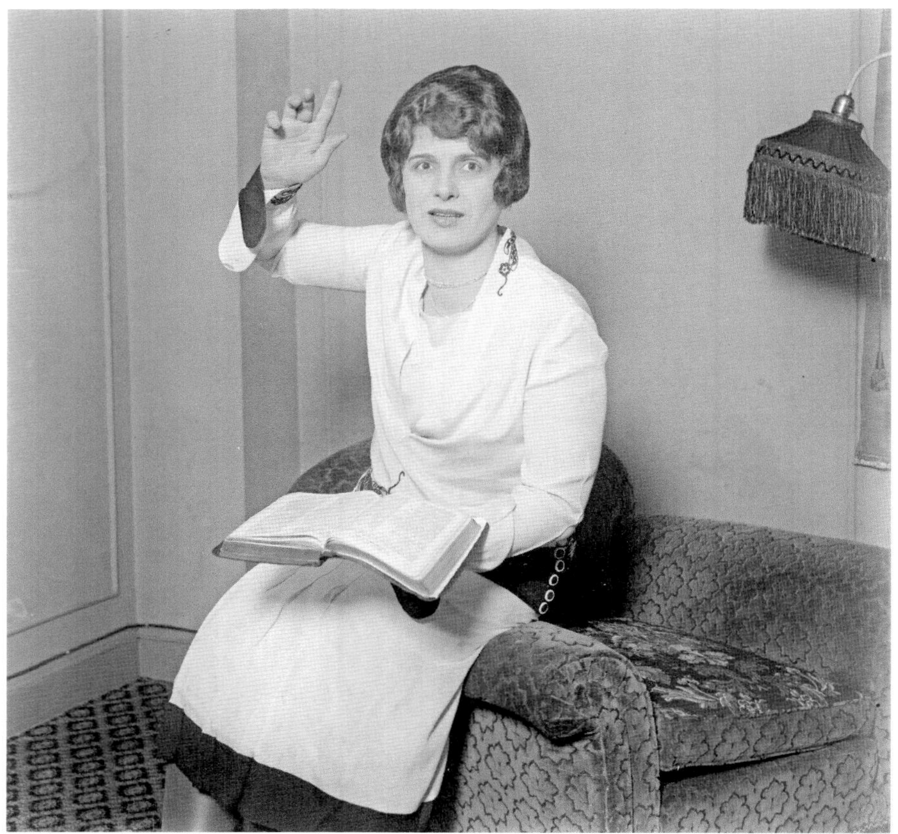

Aimee Semple McPherson. *Courtesy of the Library of Congress.*

show ran for only ninety-five performances, it garnered much notoriety because Texas wore a padlock necklace and the chorus-line dancers wore little more than padlock belts.

The highpoint of Guinan's speakeasy career and perhaps speakeasy culture occurred in 1927 when Aimee Semple McPherson, the famous Pentecostal revivalist preacher, visited New York and came to the Del Fey Club. Guinan and McPherson formed a friendship of convenience. McPherson offered a sermon, to which all in attendance bowed in reverence. She invited Guinan to attend her revival meeting at the Glad Tidings Tabernacle the next day, and Guinan, accompanied by her chorus girls, dutifully came—before going to the Del Fey for a night's adventure. "The only difference between us," Tex observed, "is that Aimee believes in the hereafter, while I want what I am here after—first."

Texas called on a group of silent partners to start yet another speak, the 300 Club on West 54th Street. In addition to her brother Tommy, her partners included the gangsters Madden, George French (aka Big Frenchy) DeMange, Nick Blair and Feet Edison; Madden also bankrolled the Cotton Club and was Dutch Schultz's rival as Gotham's top thug. Texas later ran Club Intyme in the Harding Hotel at 203–11 West 54th Street, which catered to the theater set. It became famous as an after-hours retreat for those who had spent the evening at Polly Adler's or some other nearby brothel and needed a late-night cocktail.

The police regularly raided Texas's clubs. Federal agents and local police kept inventing and enforcing new laws in a thankless effort to enforce Prohibition. These efforts ranged from new fire codes to tougher curfew enforcement. Undercover agents were often sent into clubs to buy liquor. In June 1928, 160 Prohibition agents raided 15 New York speaks. Of all those arrested, Texas was the only one who challenged her arrest.[40]

Texas's trial became a media circus. Everyone knew that Guinan ran upscale speaks and wanted her to beat the prohibitionists. Her attorney, Maxwell Lopin, skillfully manipulated the federal agents to admit during their testimony that they had a grand time at Texas's speak, repeatedly returning and spending hundreds of taxpayers' dollars on illegal booze. One agent, James L. White, said he visited the club twelve times but couldn't get in on the thirteenth because it was too crowded; he also admitted spending $360 on food and liquor. Tex was acquitted.[41]

In 1929, Texas was again busted, this time charged with "maintaining a nuisance" at yet another of her speaks, the Salon Royale. At her trial, Tex insisted that she functioned only as a hostess, serving as "a singer, dancer, welcome and wisecracker"; she sought only to bring "sunshine into the lives of tired businessmen." She described one of the stunts that the patrons enjoyed. She had "a guest walked five times around a walking cane while holding it in one hand" and then walk back to his or her table. The patron would lose his/her balance and often fall down.

The prosecutor, Norman Morrison, railed against the Guinan Graduates who performed at the Salon Royale. The exchange between Tex and the prosecutor reveals much of the spirit of the era:

> *"Those children are above reproach," Guinan insisted. "Are you trying to keep them so?" the prosecutor challenged. "I am and I do," she said. "People adore these children, and you never heard a single word against any one of them."*

"Texas Guinan on shoulders of attorney after acquittal." *Billy Rose Theatre Division, The New York Public Library Digital Collections.*

"You use the word 'sucker' often don't you?" the prosecutor pushed on.

"Yes, there are plenty of suckers. I am one of the biggest suckers in the world."

"Would you define the word 'sucker' as used in the nightclubs?"

"Oh, it is used as you would say. 'Don't be a sucker and go home so early.' It is as if you said 'pal.' It is always used in a spirit of fun and good fellowship."

Frustrated, the prosecutor told the jury: "In four months, Miss Guinan made $28,600 or thereabouts. Do you think she could have not made that not aiding and abetting?"[42]

Following a brief fifty-five-minute deliberation, the jury acquitted Texas. In the courtroom, in true Roaring Twenties' spirit, someone yelled, "Give the little girl a great big hand." At a gala victory party held at her Club Intyme, she read a telegram from Congressman (and soon-to-be mayor) Fiorello La Guardia, "Congratulations. We all give the little girl a great big hand."

2
SPEAKEASY CITY

The Place to Be

Al Hirschfeld, Broadway's legendary caricaturist long remembered for his famous sketches with his daughter's name, "Nina," hidden within, came of age during Prohibition. He was born in St. Louis in 1903 and died in Gotham a century later. He came to New York as a child, living near the Polo Grounds in the Bronx and, as a teen, attended the Vocational School for Boys, located at 138th Street and Lennox Avenue, in the heart of Harlem. Looking back on his youth, he recollected, "Harlem was as familiar and accessible to me as the blocks around your house, or the field around your homestead, or the ice floes around your igloo."[43] He attended the Art Students League and journeyed to Europe in the mid-1920s to further his studies. Retuning to Gotham, he came to intimately know Manhattan's speakeasy scene.

"At a speakeasy," Hirschfeld acknowledged, "you had to be known to get in…each place had its own clientele." Membership cards, really fake IDs, were common. "I had a couple of hundred of them," he recalled. "Some were three-dimensional, a little ball-and-chain; some of them were keys with which you opened the door; but most were just cards." And then there was the proverbial password. "Usually the password was 'Buzz,'" Hirschfeld admitted. "You'd press the button, the guy would open the little window in the door, and you'd say, 'Buzz.' And he'd open the door."[44]

Alfred Hirschfeld, caricaturist, Carl Van Vechten, 1955. *Library of Congress Prints & Photographs Online Catalog (PPOC), LOT 12735, no. 514 [P&P].*

Hirschfeld found three things common to city speaks: corruption, great music and cocktails. "Prohibition brought in the gangster era and made the whole country corrupt," he once told an interviewer, Neil Grauer. "That was the culture of the city. If you wanted to hear good swing, or anything, you had to go to a speakeasy. Anybody you can mention, from Louis Armstrong to Bix Beiderbecke, performed in speakeasies. They were all illegal, so everybody was corrupted. They all became lawbreakers."

Hirschfeld's wonderful Prohibition-era collection of caricature portraits, *The Speakeasies of 1932* (with text by Gordon Kahn and originally published in 1932 as *Manhattan Oasis*), is a drinking person's guide to three dozen popular, if illegal, Manhattan hideaways and the specialty alcoholic concoction renowned at each. As he recalled, "I interviewed all the bartenders, and the bartender would give me his favorite cocktail." But, as he honestly admitted, he only drank beer. "It was safer," he warned. "I never trusted the liquor. They always had bad liquor. Jack and Charlie's [21 club] was about the only place where you could trust your life to it."

The cocktail has a long and uncertain history. According to one rather apocryphal account, in 1779, Betsy Flanagan, a widow of a Revolutionary War soldier, opened an inn in Yorktown, New York, site of George Washington's famous 1781 battle. The inn was popular with both American and French soldiers, but the innkeeper had an ongoing tiff with a nearby English chicken farmer. As the story goes, the inn was crowded one evening when Flanagan proudly served a full-course chicken dinner. Gathering for an after-meal drink at the bar, the innkeeper offered a specially prepared concoction sporting a chicken's tail feathers. Flanagan's patrons drank festively all night, repeatedly calling for more "cock tails."[45]

The more traditional history of the cocktail traces its lineage to the early nineteenth century. The term *cocktail* appears to have been first used in 1803 in *The Farmer's Cabinet*, reporting that one Burnham "Drank a glass of cocktail—excellent for the head...Call'd at the Doct's. found Burnham—he looked very wise—drank another glass of cocktail." Three years later, the *Balance and Columbian Repository*, of Hudson, New York, defined the drink as follows:

> *Cocktail is a stimulating liquor composed of spirits of any kind, sugar, water, and bitters—it is vulgarly called a bittered sling and is supposed to be an excellent electioneering potion, inasmuch as it renders the heart stout and bold, at the same time that it fuddles the head. It is said, also to be of great use to a Democratic candidate: because a person, having swallowed a glass of it, is ready to swallow anything else.*[46]

The cocktail continued to mature throughout the nineteenth century. One thread of its lore involves the legendary San Francisco barkeep Jeremiah P. Thomas. Thomas, aka the Professor, grew up in Sackets Harbor, New York, near Lake Ontario, and traveled extensively throughout the United States, with stays in New Orleans, St. Louis, Chicago and Charleston, mastering the art of mixology. Following others seeking their fortune from the California gold rush, Thomas settled in the city by the bay landing a job as a bartender and bar manager at the Occidental Hotel. In 1851, he again relocated, this time to New York City and, in 1862, penned *The Bar-Tender's Guide*, which is still available. In it, he offered a recipe for the Martinez, consisting of Old Tom gin, Martini and Rossi sweet vermouth, a dash of maraschino and bitters, as well as a slice of lemon and two dashes of gum syrup. Thus, the martini was born.

Like the cocktail, the cocktail party seems to have originated in the United States. The first such gathering was hosted by Clara Walsh, wife of Julius S. Walsh Jr., in May 1917, and took place at their residence at 4510 Lindell Boulevard, St. Louis, Missouri. Clara Walsh invited fifty guests to her house for a one-hour Sunday afternoon fete. As originally reported, "the party scored an instant hit," and in no time, cocktail parties became "a St. Louis institution." By the '20s, it was an all-American social occasion.[47] Over time, the afternoon get-together was replaced by more formal evening events. These invitation-only get togethers pioneered the light meal or appetizer combined with imbibing alcoholic drinks, which, according to historian Catherine Gilbert Murdock, "facilitated interaction between men and women."[48]

Hirschfeld was a modern flaneur who enjoyed discovering the hidden treasures of Gotham's club life. From Jack and Charlie's, he wandered downtown to some of the Bowery's more notorious joints, where, at O'Leary's, he found a bartender offering a drink called Smoke made from Sterno. O'Leary gave careful instructions how to prepare his unique concoction:

> *Dissolve two cans of Sterno in boiling water. Stir until lumps disappear. Continue boiling for 15 minutes, add water to taste. While mixture is cooling, tear cardboard shoe box in two inch squares and drop into liquid. This draws out any poisons supposed to lurk in the mixture. Remove cardboard after 15 minutes, add a liberal pinch of tobacco for coloring. Let stand until cool. But for God's sake don't drink it.*[49]

New York mayor James Walker; cropped from photo of Walker with Umberto Nobile, *New York World-Telegram and the Sun* staff photographer. *Library of Congress Prints and Photographs Division, cph 3c21525.*

As Hirschfeld warned, "I don't know how anybody survived it." He also visited the Bath Club, the Epicure Club, Tony's, the Press Grill, the Mansion, the Place and even the uptown Cotton Club.

At these and other speaks, Hirschfeld liked rubbing shoulders with a diverse assortment of Gotham's finest—and a wide assortment of the less than finest. At the 21 club, he saw Mayor Walker, Police Commissioner Grover (aka "Gardenia") Whalen and members of the Algonquin set, be it Robert Benchley, Dorothy Parker or Heywood Broun. "Jack and Charlie were wonderful hosts and served the best liquor in town," he reminisced. He also saw the secret vault where they hid their hooch, which writer Grauer said was "hidden behind a two-and-a-half-ton brick-covered door opened by a slim piece of wire."

Chumley's, 86 Bedford Street, a cloudy morn. *Wikimedia Commons.*

Hirschfeld regularly visited Chumley's, one of Greenwich Village's legendary nightspots. "I knew Chumley, yes." Leland Stanford Chumley founded the speakeasy in 1922, during Prohibition's first phase. Located at 86 Bedford Street, it was originally a speak and a gambling den that, most recently, was renovated for twenty-first-century partygoers. One unconfirmed story claims that its address inspired the popular concept, being "86-ed" or "kill it," or, as Johnny Depp immortalized in the movie, *Donnie Brasco*, the saying, "forget about it."[50] It was, nevertheless, a longtime home to such literary notables as Scott Fitzgerald, William Faulkner, John Steinbeck, Ernest Hemingway, Allen Ginsberg and Norman Mailer. According to Grauer, Hirschfeld recalled that Chumley "was a very active political power in the Village, apart from being a very generous proprietor. He had a great following of people that would only go to Chumley's."

In 1929, the *New York Telegram* asked provocatively, "Where on Manhattan Island can you buy liquor?" Its answer tells the story of Prohibition's failure:

> *In open saloons, restaurants, nightclubs, bars behind a peephole, dancing academies, drugstores, delicatessens, cigar stores, confectionaries, soda fountains, behind petitions in shoeshine parlors, back rooms of barber shops,*

> *from hotel bellhops, from hotel headwaiters, from hotel day clerks, night clerks, in express offices, in motorcycle delivery agencies, paint stores, malt shops, cider stubs, fruit stands, vegetable markets, taxi drivers, groceries, smoke shops, athletic clubs, grillrooms, taverns, chophouses, importing firms, tearooms, moving van companies, spaghetti houses, boarding houses, Republican clubs, Democratic clubs, laundries, social clubs, newspapermen's associations.*[51]

For those who wanted to have a good time and a drink, there was no problem getting an illegal alcoholic beverage. The November 3, 1929 *Sunday News* noted that a "stranger who plans a complete tour of the night club circuit should know the following at least." Popular speakeasy lingo included *boodle* (a lot of anything), *dicty* (an upper-class person), *dogs* (feet), *getting high* (getting drunk), *juice joint* (a speak), *lap* (liquor), *spruce* (a sucker) and *working moll* (a sex worker).[52] The real message of Prohibition was simple: Drink up!

Drinking alcoholic beverages is an established aspect of the daily life of generations of Americans, especially men, and the lives of both men and women today. Taverns, eateries and homes throughout the country have, for centuries, welcomed the public and the private consumption of liquid intoxicants. However, effective 12:01 a.m. on January 16, 1920, Americans were barred from manufacturing, importing, distributing or selling intoxicating liquids.

Loopholes in federal prohibition law permitted Americans to continue to produce some traditional alcoholic beverages (cider, wine and near beer) for personal consumption and religious sacraments. It also permitted the manufacture and sale of what was understood to be industrial and medicinal alcohols, highly contaminated concoctions for non-drinking purposes but could be, with the right know-how, reprocessed into intoxicating—and sometimes deathly—beverages. These loopholes were one of the factors that undermined Prohibition's noble intentions. Temperance was intended to end the liquor trade, close down the notorious saloon and curtail the personal consumption of intoxicating beverages. Unfortunately, the compromises required to pass the Eighteenth Amendment and to implement the Volstead Act made Prohibition the greatest legislative failure in American history.

ROAR '20S, ROAR

The Roaring Twenties is remembered today as the age of the speakeasy, with its irrepressible flappers, hip flask–toting slummers, jazz bands, tough gangsters and illegal booze. Popular entertainment did much to fashion this image. Francis Coppola's *The Godfather* saga and *The Cotton Club* as well as TV series from the *Untouchables* to *Boardwalk Empire* and Ken Burns's PBS series *Prohibition* cultivated an image of the '20s in all its slick, over-the-top wildness, its Weimar-on-the-Hudson sensibility. Like Germany's Weimar Republic, the decade was an era of social delight and looming crisis.

The criminalization of liquor drove many respectable middle-class establishments out of business and resulted in the virtual criminalization of most nightlife. The proliferation of illegal speakeasies and nightclubs led to the wholesale corruption of the legal system. The buying off of local police, judges, politicians and financiers helped make the enterprise succeed. It launched some of today's great fortunes, including the Bronfmans and Kennedys. It fueled the development of crime syndicates that continue to run America's underground economy.

The historian George Chauncey points out that "the speakeasies eroded the boundaries between respectability and criminality, between public and private, and between commercial space and home life." At the speakeasy, a virtual "criminalized demimonde," patrons "entered an intimate theater in which they were expected to play a role." The intimate theater of speakeasy culture promoted the democratization of illegal and illicit behavior. Slumming had long been a privilege of well-to-do men (and some women), but speakeasy theaters allowed patrons to enjoy freer social spaces to play out their fantasies. They sometimes brought together normally disparate classes, races, ethnic groups, genders and people of diverse sexual orientations in a shared joyous transgressive setting.

As an illicit venue, a speak introduced a patron to a world of transgression. Buying a bottle at a local shop and taking it home to drink was one thing; visiting a speak and participating in the social ritual of illegal alcohol socialization was a far different thing. While one took a chance of getting arrested in a police raid, and many were busted, most patrons assumed they were safe. It was widely assumed that many local cops and federal enforcement agents were on the take. Similar to getting arrested for smoking a joint today, where one suffers only a bit of embarrassment and a fine, a police raid at a speak was for many patrons an inconvenience and, as enforcement eroded, a joke. Through payoffs, secrecy or simply invisibility, the speak provided a sense of security in which people rejected the moral imposition of Prohibition and Christian virtue. At a speak, patrons went to drink, socialize with others, enjoy themselves—and who knows what else. The speakeasy, like those run by Texas Guinan, was a venue where sin and virtue battled for the soul of America—and sin won.

House Rules

The speakeasy incubated modern American nightlife. It brought together men with money, couples out for a good time, unescorted flappers, hot music and dance, sometimes good food, gangsters and, of course, illegal drink. If a club owner was not busted by the police or squeezed dry by gangsters, there was a great deal of money to be made. According to historian Ronald Morris, market entry was relatively easy due to the high turnover rate; only a quarter of speaks were profitable during the mid-1920s, and by the late decade, three-out of four speaks had failed. He estimates that the average lifespan of a successful speak was less than thirty months, and those that survived retuned between 5 and 10 percent profit per month.[53]

The conventional speakeasy was a modest affair. It ran about twenty by one hundred feet and had a seating capacity for 125 patrons. To break even, it had to operate at 50 percent capacity. The startup costs for clubs varied depending on how glamorous they were; some clubs, Morris notes, "opened literally on shoestrings." For example, Texas Guinan's brother Tommy opened Texas Tommy at a cost of $800, while "Legs" Diamond's Hotsy Totsy Club required $1,000. Billy Rose, the legendary Broadway impresario, claimed that he earned back the initial startup costs of $4,000 for his hit club, the Back Stage, located at 110 East 56th Street, on opening night. However, entertainer Jimmy Durante and his partners ponied up an estimated $25,000 to open Club Durant, located at 232 West 58th Street.

Operating costs varied depending on the club. Cost at a modest club was pretty minimal, with salaries averaging $25 a week for a bartender and $1 a night (plus food and tips) for the waiters; unless they were leading performers at a high-end nightclub, musicians worked for tips. According to Durante, costs at his Les Ambassadeurs Club, on Broadway near 50th Street, ran as follows: orchestra at 35 percent, staff at 15 percent and rent at 10 percent; advertising, supplies and "miscellaneous losses" (such as bribes) were extra. During Prohibition's glory days of 1923–28, more spectacular revues significantly increased these costs. Margins were tight, often leading club owners not to pay their staff; in 1933, Larry Fay was offed by the doorman of his last speak, the Casa Blanca, for not paying his salary.[54]

Billy Rose acknowledged that it took a certain type of personality to run a successful speak. One had to be "wacky, a big fibber, swell-headed, bull-headed, and fat-headed."[55] No wonder speaks attracted gangsters. However, more than the illegal hooch or prostitution, numbers and other rackets drew them to speaks. Nightclubs offered gangsters social status and public prominence. If popular, the speak could be a favorite nightspot for celebrities, politicians, athletes and the well-heeled; one could get one's name and photo in newspapers. According to Morris, some gangsters also liked jazz and even played instruments.[56] More so, the speakeasy provided an opportunity for the gangsters to hire their relatives and friends; thus, people owed them.

Successful mob-run speaks relied on conventional techniques to maintain and/or increase the club's business. The principal method was word-of-mouth advertising to create a special aura about the club. This often relied on making sure sexy women, often prostitutes, were regulars as well as hosting special events like a new band or revue, offering free drinks to special customers and even canceling a rival's gambling debts.

If the gangster wanted to maintain an upscale, respectable club, he knew all too well that he and his staff had to adhere to an unstated but widely accepted code of ethics. The first principle of this code was to keep club secrets *secret*—foremost was keeping one's name hidden. This explained why gangsters often hired relatives and retained the club's more legitimate owner as a front man. The second principle was to avoid violence. As Morris insists, "The inside of a cabaret was off-limits for mobster rough stuff." Thus, no pickpockets, no knockout drugs, no muggings, no purse snatchings, no robberies. Mayhem brought bad press, police crackdowns, expensive repairs and loss of trade. Some speaks had visiting gangsters check their guns at the door. Third, and equally critical, most mob-run speaks went out of their way to safeguard women, be they staff, performers, patrons or prostitutes. "In fact," notes Morris, "clubs prided themselves on keeping women who ventured in by themselves free from annoyance." Finally, gangsters knew they had to hide the hooch if or when a police raid threatened to close them down. Thus, nearly all clubs had special escape routes, trap doors, false walls, sliding panels and alarm systems in case of a raid. Even a reputable club like the 21 invested heavily in such protection, maintaining four alarm buttons at various points in the vestibules; if a raid prevented one of them from being pushed, the doorman could reach for another. It also sported five separate liquor caches, reachable only through secret doors, and the switches were instantly short circuited whenever an alarm button was pressed. Safety features were an expensive alternative or complement to paying off public officials![57]

During Prohibition, many cops were on the take. In 1927, Joe Helbock ran the Famous Door, a jazz club at 35 West 52nd Street, and knew how the game was played. "You stayed in business only if you had enough money and the right connections," he reflected. "I had pretty good ones," he added, "one was deputy police commissioner. With them you could get the word on whom to pay and how much." A regular, Louis Vance, laid out how the bribe worked: "Before any profits could be dispersed, a thick slice must be set aside for protection—an omnibus name for 'everybody in the know,' from rum barons to the district leader of the [Democratic] party to the powerful and venal plainclothesmen that infested such clubs like flies."[58] One New York proprietor estimated his operation costs were about $1,370 a month. One-third ($400) was spent on bribes to federal Prohibition agents, police officers and city district attorney officials. In addition, the cops on the beat would get an extra $40 each to turn their backs whenever beer was delivered.

The Price of Pleasure

Charles Norris, New York's chief medical examiner during Prohibition, reported that "between October 6 and 8, 1928, twenty-five men and women died in the city of New York from wood alcohol poisoning." He pointed out that the death rate attributed to alcohol stood at 518 for the first seven months of 1928, in line with 719 for 1927, but significantly up from the 87 for 1918. He cautioned his readers that "there are therefore no reliable or trustworthy statistics in regard to fatal effects of alcohol in New York City, but it is certain that the real total is much in excess of the published figures." Carefully reframing the argument, Norris added, "These five and twenty Americans died not of poison liquor but of poisoned liquor."[59]

If one was Al Hirschfeld and went to some of the city's better speakeasies, like the 21 club, one could pretty much count on the quality of the liquor. However, he warned, you took your chances at most other speaks, especially the farther down the pecking order you went. They included the innumerable, and mostly anonymous, fly-by-night "big pigs" or "blind pigs," "shock houses" and "smoke joints" that dispensed bootlegged liquors, home-brewed bathtub drink and other illegal substances in working-class neighborhoods throughout the city. Lois Long, who wrote the Lipstick column on nightlife for the *New Yorker*, described her speakeasy days bluntly: "You never knew what you were drinking or who you'd wake up with."[60]

Poisoned liquor was one of the consequences of the compromises that enabled the passage of the Volstead Act. It permitted the manufacture and sale of what was classified as industrial and medicinal alcohols. The act also permitted individuals to produce alcohol for sacramental purposes and for their own personal consumption. This loophole led to the emergence of "urban moonshiners," people who concocted illegal hooch in their home, apartment or nearby storefront. New York hardware stores sold a one-gallon still for six or seven dollars, and some more enterprising consumers set up semicommercial stills producing bathtub gin of dubious pedigree. Two scholars, Mark Lender and James Martin, found that "'bathtub gin' got its name from the fact that alcohol, glycerin and juniper juice was mixed in bottles or jugs too tall to be filled with water from a sink tap so they were commonly filled under a bathtub tap."[61] And it could kill.

Much debate took place assessing whether Prohibition decreased alcohol consumption. Two prominent Prohibition-era economists, Irving Fisher and Clark Warburton, argued that the policy led to decreased consumption. They argued that by making liquor illegal, the price of alcohol rose significantly, which led to a decline in consumption. In 1918 (a war year), a barrel of domestic beer costs $10.50, and by the early 1920s, it had jumped to $160 a barrel; a quart of domestic spirits jumped from $1.39 a quart in 1918 to $4.00 a quart in 1930. An average cocktail cost about $0.15 in 1918; by the early '20s, it had jumped to $0.75.[62]

However, this hypothesis has come under serious criticism, most pointedly from Jeffrey Miron and Jeffrey Zwiebel. They argue that "alcohol consumption fell sharply at the beginning of Prohibition, to approximately 30 percent of its pre-Prohibition level." More telling, they stressed that by the time Prohibition was repealed, alcohol consumption had witnessed an upswing "to about 60–70 percent of its pre-Prohibition level."[63]

One of Prohibition's unanticipated consequences was a fundamental change in American's drinking habits. During the 1880s, beer and spirits (whiskey, gin, scotch and other "hard" liquors) accounted for nearly all of America's alcoholic consumption; with spirits at 47 percent, beer at 45 percent and wine at only 7 percent. On the eve of Prohibition in 1919, beer accounted for more than half (55 percent), and spirits had declined to just over one-third (37 percent). Warburton, writing in 1932, found that between 1921 and 1929, beer consumption increased 463 percent, wine by 100 percent and spirits more then fivefold. Beer consumption accounted for only 15 percent, while, by 1920, spirits made up three-fourths (75 percent) of drinking.[64]

Today, beer has an average alcoholic content—ABV, alcohol by volume—of 4 to 5 percent by volume. Before Prohibition, most beers had about 6 to 7 percent alcohol; for example, the alcohol content of Guinness is 4 percent, Sierra Nevada, 5.3 percent and Brooklyn Black Chocolate Stout, 8.3 percent. Under the Volstead Act, an alcoholic beverage was limited to an ABV of 0.5 percent by volume. Brewers attempted to circumvent the act by producing what was known as near beer with an ABV of less than the 0.5 percent. However, this beer is reported to have been quite bland in taste, leading drinkers to harder stuff. In 1921, an estimated nine million barrels of near beer was produced; by 1932, the total had shrunk by two-thirds, to less than three million. In 1927, the Prohibition Bureau estimated that Americans were making seven hundred million gallons of homebrew per year.[65]

The change in drinking patterns during the 1920s reflects what Richard Cowan identified as the "Iron Law of Prohibition." Under his hypothesis, the more severe police enforcement, the more potent the prohibited substance becomes. During Prohibition, alcoholic beverages, particularly whiskies or spirits, were produced and consumed under illegitimate market conditions. Thus, they became more potent, with uncertain variability in potency and a greater likelihood to be adulterated with unknown or dangerous substances.[66]

In the worst cases, adulterated alcohol, what New York's chief medical examiner Norris called "poisoned liquor," led to acute alcoholism and sometimes deaths. U.S. data indicates that during Prohibition, mortality rates for chronic or acute alcoholism increased steadily. Mark Thorton noted, "Cirrhosis of the liver has been found to pose a significant health risk, particularly in women who consume more than four drinks per day." He warned that "the vast majority of heavy drinkers never develop it." In 1919, the mortality from chronic or acute alcoholism rate stood at 1.6 per 100,000; the following year, it fell to 1.0 and steadily increased to 4.0 in 1927 and flattened out to 2.5 per 100,000 in 1932. This is in comparison to 7.3 per 100,000 in 1907. Deborah Blum estimated the government program led to the death of 10,000 people. To put these numbers in context, the great American wit Will Rogers reflected, "Governments used to murder by the bullet only. Now it's by the quart."[67]

The Roaring Twenties perfected the cocktail. Hirschfeld enjoyed a martini at Sam's, a Greenwich Village speakeasy on MacDougal Street. He described the venue with affection: "The room is large, nicely lighted and not overdressed. The dancing space is ample, and the booths for drinking are spacious and comfortable." The barkeep was a fellow named Tom, a sullen guy who kept his distance from the patrons. His cocktail, the martini, was simple but effective:

⅔ gin
⅓ French vermouth
(orange or angostura added if required)

Shake well and strain into cocktail glass

Sam's speak did not attract locals, who were predominately Italians. Rather, it attracted slummers, "fiction magazine editors; minor executives who took postgraduated work in light of love-making in these purlieus; a lot of young men with crisp, black mustaches, all call[ed] 'Doc.' They're dentists and not to be taken seriously."[68]

3
FROM COWGIRL TO SHOWGIRL

Texas Girl

How did Mary Louise Cecelia Guinan from Waco, Texas, born on January 12, 1884, end up the queen of Gotham's speakeasies? Her story is of a remarkable woman and the profound social developments remaking fin de siècle America.

Texas was the daughter of two Canadian parents, Michael and Bessie (Duffy) Guinan. Her four grandparents originally immigrated to Canada from Ireland in the 1840s, settling in small towns near Quebec. Her parents independently migrated to the United States, met and married in Georgetown, Colorado, on June 18, 1881. Bessie gave birth to seven children, of which five survived; Tex was the first girl and Tommy (born in 1891) would follow her to New York and the speakeasy life.[69]

In the late nineteenth century, Waco was a center of economic opportunity. The county had a population of sixty thousand and was the northern terminus of the San Antonio and Aransas Pass Railroad. It claimed ten banks and several newspapers; a dozen flour, wool and cotton-seed mills; numerous cotton and canning factories; six hundred farms producing cotton; and hog, sheep, cattle and horse ranching. Texas's father, Michael, together with two partners, formed a wholesale grocery business that ultimately failed, just one of his unsuccessful ventures.[70]

The Guinans were Catholics in a Baptist town, and Mary Louise attended Waco's Convent School of Sacred Heart. According to family lore, she got her nickname, "Texas," from a family friend when just a kid. As a child, Texas's biographer, Louise Berliner, reported, "she was a wild, harum-scarum tomboy who climbed trees with the boys and played pranks on the townspeople and the nuns at the convent where she went to school."[71]

As she forged her remarkable career as an entertainer—in theater, the movies and at grand Gotham speaks—Guinan loved to tell tall tales about her childhood and youth. One of her apocryphal tales claimed that she grew up on a farm where she learned to ride and shoot. According to Berliner and others, she actually was raised in town, first at 1436 Washington Street and later at 604 North 4th. Tex also claimed she got her first theatrical experience performing in Saturday matinees at the Waco Opera House. Berliner kindly points out: "I concluded that Tex didn't exactly rewrite the past, just reimagined it, shuffling the pieces a little. This was the childhood that fit, that matched the spirit and what she became." She adds, "The little cowgirl was never once called Mayme, always Little Tex or Tomboy Texas, a miniature night-club hostess in training."[72] Nevertheless, she did learn to ride a horse and shoot a gun.

Her father's business failure in Waco led the family to move to Denver, Colorado, in 1900, and it is there that she first became interested in theater. She regularly visited the Church of Immaculate Conception's social and fashion shows. In Denver, she met John—nicknamed "Johnny," "Jack" or "Moy"—Moynahan, a cartoonist for the *Rocky Mountain News*. They eloped and were married on December 2, 1904, when she was twenty years old. She signed the marriage license "Marie."[73]

In 1905, the couple moved to Chicago when Moynahan got a better job at the *Chicago Examiner*; the following year, they relocated to Cleveland because Moy got a still better job with the *Cleveland News*. In Cleveland, Marie sang with a local church choir and performed at a small café. According to Berliner, all changed one evening when the couple attended a performance by the entertainer Charlotte Walker, a Broadway actress and early movie star, who inspired the soon-to-be-Texas with a sense of creative possibility.[74] The couple returned to Chicago when Jack got a better job. During this period, the couple grew apart. As Berliner notes, "The role of housewife had lost its novelty. Eventually, the desire for a career would compel Marie to choose between Moy and the stage."

Opposite: Texas Guinan portrait. *Billy Rose Theatre Division, The New York Public Library Digital Collections.*

Above: Charlotte Walker. *Wikimedia Commons.*

SHOWGIRL SHUFFLE

While living in Chicago, Guinan met Reginald De Koven, a well-known musical composer, who invited her to visit him when she was in New York. Little did he expect her to take him up on his offer. After her divorce, Tex moved to New York in 1907. Upon arrival, she went to De Koven's house at 42 East 66th Street, and—as the story goes—she walked in on a dinner party, exclaiming, "Hello, Mr. De Koven, I'm here at last." Flummoxed, De Koven welcomed her as an invitee, sat her among his guests (Tex claims Enrico Caruso, the great Italian operatic tenor, was there) and—eventually—realized who she was. He then invited her to visit his office the next day. He gave Texas her first job in his operetta *The Snowman*, a "pictorial musical," the latest in vaudeville style. She was featured in an act called "The Gibson Girl" and undertook a road tour that eventually opened for a short run in New York as *The Girls of Holland*. *Variety* panned her performance, warning, "Perhaps if Miss Guinan would relax just a trifle upon her very distinct enunciation for the benefit of her voice, she would more fully justify the special mention on the program."[75]

Upon her arrival in Gotham, Guinan settled in Greenwich Village, taking a room at 72 Washington Square at two dollars a week. She would remain a Village resident for the rest of her life and, in time, own a luxurious seven-room apartment at 17 West 8th Street. During the early twentieth century, the Village was the center of an emerging bohemian scene that included the well-to-do like Gertrude Vanderbilt Whitney who opened a sculpture gallery in an old stable. It was home to writers Eugene O'Neill, Edna St. Vincent Millay, John Dos Passos and Willa Cather as well as anarchists John Reed and Emma Goldman. Texas had a love affair with John Warren, a "stage-door Johnnie," that Berliner identifies as the "first of many 'younger' men to flow in and out of Tex's life, men who seemed motivated by mercenary intentions behind their professed love."[76]

In May 1909, Guinan performed as the "Lone Star Novelty" at the Keith and Proctor's Fifth Avenue Theatre suspended seven feet above the stage and singing popular songs. Later that year, she was cast by John P. Slocum, a musical-comedy producer, as the lead in *The Gay Musician*, which was so successful that it led them to form a partnership. They apparently had a nonsexual relationship in which Slocum was more like a father figure; Stein warned, "Slocum spoiled Texas." In late November, she appeared in Los Angeles, and the *Los Angeles Times* gave her a mixed review: "Miss Texas Guinan is in the budding prima donna stage.…[S]he should appear to be more in the play if she would address herself more to the people of the stage and less to the front." While in Los Angeles, she hooked up with an old lover, Julian Johnson (nicknamed "JJ"), who got her a job with the Oliver Morosco Theatrical Enterprises, a stock company. Berliner observes, JJ "was the great romance that all heroines were supposed to experience at least once in their story."[77]

Over the next few years, while living and working in Gotham, Guinan traveled extensively, performing throughout the Midwest and Canada. In the fall of 1912, she was to perform in the Schuberts' *The Passing Show of 1912* but was—as Berliner notes—"fat," and the Schuberts forced her to go on a serious diet. In June 1913, she visited her hometown of Denver, where she gave a popular lecture about horseback riding; in Canada, she paraded on horseback riding astride instead of sidesaddle, scandalizing the public. On Thanksgiving Eve, she opened in *O' My Thumb*, a British import, at the Manhattan Opera House.

In July 1913, she returned to New York exhausted and suffering from a fever and collapsed twice at home. Recuperating in Los Angeles, she met Walter Cunningham, who was promoting the Marjorie Hamilton Obesity Cure. He purchased Lillian Russell's "anti-fat remedy" and partnered with Texas, incorporating as Texas Guinan Inc. Texas served as the promotional star, while Cunningham ran the company; an ad accompanied by a photo of Texas read, "God's masterpiece and the most fascinating actress in America." Cunningham appears to have changed the original formula, and numerous complaints were raised, drawing the attention of the American Medical Association and the U.S. Post Office. In September, the AMA undertook a formal investigation, and in January 1914, the Post Office found Tex was part of a "scheme for obtaining money through the mails by means of false and fraudulent pretenses, representations and promises." It ceased her mail delivery related to the product.[78]

Hollywood Cowgirl

In 1917, Guinan was performing at the Winter Garden Theatre and had convinced the manager to let her ride a horse down the runway instead of simply dancing. Riding a snow-white charger, she was "all dressed up in black lace chaps and swinging a lariat." She was "discovered" by a scout for the Balboa Amusement Production Company and was signed to a two-reel western, *The Wildcat,* released May 3, 1917.

In '17, Texas also signed with Yonkers-based Triangle Film Corporation, an early Hollywood studio based in Culver City, California, along with her "husband," JJ. Triangle was formed in 1915 by Mack Sennett (comedy), D.W. Griffith (drama) and Thomas H. Ince (westerns). It was backed by Harry and Roy Aiken, and she convinced them to let her play—as biographer Glenn Shirley says—"an authentic lady gunslinger on the celluloid prairie."[79] Her first film was *The Fuel of Life,* directed by Walter Edwards and released in November 1917 to mixed reviews. It was followed by *The Gun Woman,* starring William S. Hart, the leading western movie star during the silent film era. Texas was cast as "Tigress," and, as Berliner notes, she "was one of the first women to enter what had previously been male territory." She adds, "Throughout the next five years, 1918–1922, she [Guinan] would create a new role for the women in film—that of the woman who was self-reliant in every crisis and could handle a six-shooter like a man." Most critical, Berliner concludes, "Tex was a bad woman with a good heart."

In 1918, Texas reportedly signed with Frohman Amusement Corporation in a deal to star in twenty-six two-reel "dramatic features typifying the glories and hazards of the women of the Great West…to be released one every two weeks."[80] The first release was *The She Wolf,* which consists of 6,700 feet of film and was released in five reels. Shirley considers the Frohman two-reel release *Little Miss Deputy* "one of Guinan's best pictures." As he explains, "Playing the part of a deputy sheriff, she is placed in a situation where she must either renounce her womanhood and hang the man she loves or take off her badge. She proves that the hero has been wrongly accused and saves him at the critical moment."[81] Frohman advertised a "26 two reel dramatic feature productions typifying the rights, glories and hazards of the women of the Great West" starring Guinan.

Lobby card for *The Gun Woman* (1919) with Texas Guinan. *Wikimedia Commons.*

Top: *The She Wolf*, from *Moving Picture World*, May 1919. *Wikimedia Commons.*

Bottom: Advertisement, *Moving Picture World*, May 1919, for films with actress Texas Guinan. *Internet Archive.*

The following year, she signed with Bulls-Eye Studio (taken over by Reelcraft) and worked on a series of twelve two-reelers directed by Jay Hart that included *The Lady and the Law* and *My Lady Robin Hood*. However, two of the films received complaints from censorship boards in Pennsylvania and Michigan. A year later, she signed with Victor Kramer Productions for two films directed by Francis Ford, *I Am the Woman* and *The Stampede*. She also stars in *Boss of the Rancho* (1919).

Left: *Boss of the Rancho*, 1919. *Wikimedia Commons*.

Below: *White House* (*Cow Girl*) in 1922. *Left to right*: Harold Vosburgh, George Nagle, Miss Guinan, Arthur Ludwig, Wells Guinan, April 22, 1922. *Library of Congress, Digital ID 2016832487*.

In 1920, Al Jolson recruited Guinan to the Harding and Coolidge Theatrical League to back the presidential campaign of Republican Warren Harding. In August, she traveled to Marion, Ohio, to attend a fundraiser for Harding; Guinan sat next to Florence Harding and was, according to reports, "well-behaved." Following the election, she traveled through the South with Niles Granlund. In '22, she was performing in Washington, D.C., when Harding came to the theater to see her show. When her performance ended, the president-elect stood in his box and thanked Texas for her support during the campaign. To the applause of those in the audience, he said "he hoped he would be as good a President as Texas Guinan was an entertainer."[82] As history would show, he was not.

In August 1921, she set up Texas Guinan Productions and leased the Fine Arts Studio on Sunset Boulevard, where Griffith's *Birth of a Nation* was filmed. She released five two-reel westers, including *The Spitfire*, *The Heart of Texas* and *Texas of the Mounted*; in *Texas of the Mounted*, she plays the dual roles of twin brother and sister. She also sold vending machine cards and perforated gummed stamps with her picture on them. Texas also appeared in *White House* (*Cow Girl*) in 1922 and *Night Rider* (1929).

Unfortunately, as Shirley admits, "the day of the 'quickie' western was waning."[83] Guinan made a total of thirty-six films, three of them talkies.[84] She returned to Gotham in 1922.

4
PARTY TIME IN THE WET ZONE

Roaring Twenties Gotham

In the 1920s, New York's population stood at 5.6 million—it was America's capital city. Unfortunately, no one knows the true number of speakeasies operating in the city during Prohibition. One 1925 estimate speculates that there were over 100,000; in 1929, the police commissioner reported only 32,000 "resorts" serving alcohol throughout the city. No matter how many speaks, all agreed that the epicenter of America's speakeasy universe was midtown Manhattan's Theatre District, the "wet zone." It was clustered from 45th to 56th Streets and from Madison Avenue on the Eastside west through Broadway to 8th Avenue. In this urban bazaar, any New Yorker or visitor could stroll into almost any building and purchase liquor, but for a good time, those in need of a drink went to a quality speak.

New York speakeasies ranged from fashionable nightclubs to low-life haunts. Wet zone clubs included popular cabarets run by Texas Guinan and other celebrities. There were dance clubs like Roseland, featuring Louis Armstrong, and the Kentucky Club, where Duke Ellington got his start. The wet zone was also home to drinking clubs like the Pen and Pencil and Artists and Writers. Still other popular speaks that dotted the area included: on 49th Street, the Chesterfield Inn and Tony's, operated by Tony Gerdello. On 52nd Street was the Biarritz, Furnace Club, the Onyx and Tony Soma's Tony's. On 53rd Street there was the Don Juan and the Park View Club; on

Broadway theaters, 1920. *Wikimedia Commons.*

54th Street and Broadway, the Hotsy Totsy Club; on 55th Street, the Tree Club; and on 56th Street, the Long Cabin, Back Stage Club, Merry-Go-Round and the Hi Hat.

Prohibition not only put an end to the legal sale of alcohol but also forced the closing of many of city's most celebrated dining or lobster palaces. These included Rector's, Reisenweber's, Maxim's, Churchill's and, most especially, Delmonico's, which has opened in 1837. In the 1920s as well as today, restaurants, upscale or local eateries, depend on the sale of alcohol to supplement the limited margins on food. As Prohibition took effect, many upscale eateries went bankrupt.

Nevertheless, as Prohibition became institutionalized in the mid-20s, smart businessmen and opportunistic gangsters opened a new set of upscale restaurant speaks. Chefs at these party palaces required alcohol in the preparation of their quality meals. How could one have a good meal without a before-dinner cocktail, a fine wine with the entrée and an aperitif with dessert? The trickle of booze in the kitchen became a flood in the dining room. Among these upscale dining clubs were the Stork Club and the Silver Slipper—alcohol supplied by the "Broadway Mob" of Joe Adonis and Frank Costello—and the 21 club. Fancy supper clubs also included the Plantation, where Ethel Waters, Florence Mills and Josephine Baker performed. Swank restaurants joined fashionable nightclubs in the wet zone as destinations for those with the money to have a good time and who had no problem breaking the law.

Most of Manhattan's exclusive speaks, like Texas's El Fey club, were clustered in the wet zone. Each had its own ambiance and cultivated its own clientele. For example, Tony Soma's, located on West 52nd Street near 6th Avenue, was a popular spot for the legendary Algonquin Round Table group of writers. Frank Case, who ran the Algonquin Hotel, kept it dry, but this did not stop the members of the Round Table group from having a little inebriated fun nearby. At Tony's, the bartender is said to have asked Dorothy Parker: "What are you having?" She quipped, "Not much fun." (Texas didn't socialize with the Round Table crowd because, as a wit observed, she didn't do lunch.)

Club Alabam, located in the basement of the 44th Street Theatre Building at 216 West 44th Street, was one of the first wet zone nightspots to feature Black musicians. The first revue was the Creole Follies, featuring Edith Wilson and Fletcher Henderson and His Famous Club Alabam Orchestra. (Wilson was an African American vaudeville and blues performer, who, after World War II, was cast by the Quaker Oats Company as "Aunt Jemima" for advertisements, radio and television performances.) One of the city's earliest local radio stations, WHN, regularly ran a wire into the club, and its broadcasts were, according to radio historian, Philip Eberly, "one of radio's first outlets for a Negro band."[85]

The 21 was one of the Prohibition era's most famous dinner clubs. It began inauspiciously as the Red Head, a little basement blind pig in Greenwich Village opened in 1922 by two entrepreneurial cousins, Jack

21 Club, 2006. *Creative Commons/Wikimedia Commons.*

Kriendler and Charlie Berns. They got their start running soft drink and pony ride concessions in Catskill resorts, and their first speak, like many others served food: ham and cheese sandwiches during the week, steak and eggs on the weekends.[86]

After fire destroyed their first speak, Jack and Charlie opened another Village spot, Club Fronton. From there, it was just a hop-skip-jump uptown to West 49th Street, where they launched the Puncheon Grotto in 1926 for the college crowd. In the wake of the 1929 stock market crash, Jack and Charlie moved their fourth club into the basement of an elegant brownstone at 21 West 52nd Street, naming the speak 21.[87] It was the first speakeasy opened on a residential block and was a true success. Sensing that Prohibition was going to end, they repositioned their club by offering better wines and liquors to serve more discriminating patrons. And the discriminating gentry flocked to the 21.

Jack and Charlie became established figures on Broadway. Jack, especially, exemplified the spirit of the Roaring Twenties. Born John Carl Kriendler, an Austrian immigrant, Jack assumed a distinct place among the Broadway set. He was, put simply, a snob. His elegant, if unpretentious, wardrobe and manners landed him the moniker "the Baron"—and he later married a Belgian baroness. However, his greatest pleasure came from donning fancy cowboy outfits and running a dude ranch, which earned him the nickname "Two-Trigger Jack."

Hirschfeld regularly visited the 21 and reported that Bill, the barkeep, offered a special cocktail, Gin Daisy, which consisted of:

⅔ gin
1/6 Cointreau
1/6 lemon juice

Add grenadine. Serve over cracked ice with fruit ornamentation.

As many of its patrons have reported, the 21 served good food. Hirschfeld agreed: "The cuisine is a happy wedding of the British and French. A five-dollar bill will see you through on the meal check, but you'll resolve to go for a ten the next time."[88] However, he admitted to Grauer that the high prices were intended to keep out "the riffraff, the curious, by charging outrageous prices—twenty dollars for lunch!" And in 1932, $20 was real money, equivalent by one estimate to $314 in purchasing power today.[89]

During Prohibition, Jack and Charlie's clubs, like those of Texas Guinan, were targets of numerous police raids. The 21 developed an ingenious scheme to protect their illegal goods. Jack and Charlie equipped the club with four alarm buttons at various points in the entrance vestibule, enabling the doorman to hit multiple alarms when confronted by Prohibition agents. The club also had five separate liquor caches, reachable only through secret doors. Each had an electrical switch that, when an alarm button was pressed, would short circuit the cache door. In 2020, the 21 celebrated its ninety-first anniversary.[90]

The Stork Club is another Prohibition-era legend. The first club was opened in 1929 at 132 West 58th Street—and quite by accident. John Sherman Billingsley—known to all as "Sherm"—loved the limelight and, although married, was a notorious stage door Romeo. He was talked into opening the club in partnership with two acquaintances from Oklahoma, who, like him, were small-time gangsters who'd come to Gotham seeking their fortunes. Sherm had arrived a few years earlier from Detroit and settled in the Bronx, where he ran a chain of lucrative pharmacies that dispensed medicinal alcohol and other curatives.[91]

Taking a lease to properties at 132 West 58th Street, the partners found it tough going, and the two Oklahomans decided to go home. They sold their interest to a mysterious investor, one Thomas Healy, who wanted only a 30 percent stake in the venture and to function as a silent partner. Sherm soon discovered that his silent partner represented none other than the notorious Madden gang. When Billingsley attempt to break the deal, one of the gangsters informed him: "We didn't pay $10,000 for an interest in the business. We paid ten for a 30 percent interest in everything you do for the rest of your life." So much for silent partners.

Sherm claimed he was one of nine children, born in the backroom of a grocery store at a deserted railroad stop in Enid, Oklahoma. He joked that Enid was *dine* spelled backward and claimed that he got his start in the liquor trade selling to Native Americans when he was seven years old. However, he often failed to mention his stay at Leavenworth Penitentiary for bootlegging or that many of his original partners were gangsters.

Billingsley was temperamental, often arbitrary and tyrannical. He regularly barred customers from the Stork for real or imaginary reasons. Some patrons complained that Sherm refused them entry because they had been photographed at another swank nightspot or for carrying matches from another club. He routinely fired help for no apparent reason. Stories circulated (especially in the 1950s) that he'd installed electronic eavesdropping equipment in some of the club's rooms, including the kitchen, check room and the entrance to the Cub Room and that he recorded telephone conversations.

Nevertheless, Sherm and the Stork Club were Broadway icons until it closed in 1965. Early on, Sherm regularly visited Guinan's clubs, and when he had trouble filling the house during its difficult early days, Texas sent the young gossip columnist Walter Winchell over to do a story on the newest, hottest spot in the city. The story put the Stork Club on the map. However, Prohibition agents repeatedly closed it down. After one raid, Sherm moved the club to 51½ East 51st Street; then, in 1934, to 3 East 53rd Street, where it remained a fixture of café society for decades.

Originally popular with the theater crowd, the Stork Club later appealed to debutantes and the college set. The younger crowd often came from upper-crust families, lending glamour to the speak. Sherm gained popularity by hosting special events, including raffles and "balloon nites" decorated with balloons that hid $100 bills inside, and offering gifts such as suspenders and neckties to male patrons and gold compacts to females. He is reported to have given diamond-studded bracelets to his special favorites.

Stork Club's Cub Room, November 1944. *From left*: Orson Welles (with cigar), Margaret Sullavan with husband, owner Sherman Billingsley (center table at far right), Morton Downey (at right); photo by Alfred Eisenstaedt, *Life Magazine*. *Wikipedia Commons*.

The Cub Room—disparaged as the "Snub Room" by those excluded—was the site of the most celebrated and exclusive part of the Stork Club. It was the club's inner sanctum, located just inside the front door and separated by an allegedly solid gold chain. Only Sherm's best customers got in, and of course, they included anybody with fame, fortune or a gun in their pocket. Over the years, the Stork offered fine food that emphasized French cuisine. It most famous contribution to popular dining was the chicken hamburger: boned and ground chicken mixed with salt, pepper, nutmeg, butter, heavy cream and breadcrumbs. It was served with tomato sauce, French-fried sweet potatoes and buttered green peas. It became a late-night delicacy.

WOMEN AND SPEAKS

Speakeasies were a historical accident. They were a commercial innovation by clever businessmen and gangsters, with the complicity of politicians and police, to redress what they, and millions of ordinary people, believed to be the illegitimate imposition of a conservative moral value, abstinence, on all Americans.

Speaks evolved out of New York's changing nightlife entertainment culture. The half century of industrialization following the Civil War

Helen Morgan. Black and white photography Carl Van Vechten (1935). *Courtesy of the Library of Congress.*

transformed America, catapulting Gotham into the nation's first metropolis and spawning a vital and innovative entertainment scene. Lewis Erenberg, in *Stepping Out*, masterfully chronicles the city's transformation between 1890 and 1930, linking innovations in popular culture such as dance, music, theater, nightclub performance and movies to changes in gender relations, moral values and notions of personal pleasure, sexual and otherwise.[92] In particular, this transition witnessed the evolution of female entertainer from burlesque to vaudeville, from cabaret to nightclub and, most importantly for speakeasy nightlife, from chorus girl to hostess.

Texas was not the only woman to preside over a speak. Helen Morgan was a former Ziegfeld girl, nightclub performer, early torch singer and Broadway and movie star. She is most remembered today, eight decades later, for the scandalous role she plays as a mulatto opposite Paul Robeson in the theatrical and movie production of *Show Boat*. She opened Chez Morgan in 1927 and became a front-page celebrity when Prohibition agents busted her speak, finding only twenty-five bottles of alcohol but causing $75,000 worth of damage. After much rancor, the charges were dropped. She then opened Summer Home and was arrested again, but a jury trial acquitted her. After the repeal of Prohibition, she opened the legendary House of Morgan. Other posh nightspots run by women were Belle Livingstone's Country Club and Gilda Gray's Piccadilly Rendezvous.

The female theatrical performer—and, indirectly, the American woman—was increasingly sexualized in the decades following the Civil War. Burlesque made its U.S. debut in New York City during the evening of September 28, 1868, when British star Lydia Thompson took the stage of George Wood's Broadway Theatre to perform in *Ixion*. At the 1893 Chicago Exposition, Little Egypt (Ashea Wabe) and Fatima (Fahreda Mahzar) performed erotic dances that fulfilled White male fantasies about the erotic temptations of the "primitive" woman. The "girl show" first appeared as a sideshow at the 1893 Chicago Exposition and quickly became a feature of touring carnivals, bringing live entertainment to small-town and rural America throughout the country. Between 1902 and 1920, the number of girl shows operating across the United States jumped from seventeen to an estimated two hundred.

By the time of the 1893 Chicago Exposition, the Bowery burlesque became increasingly one-dimensional, moving more and more toward sexual explicitness with female performers incorporating the belly dance, fan dance and, in its more extreme expression, the "cooch" or "hootchy-kootchy" dance. In 1917, May Dix crossed the invisible line, performing the first strip at the Minsky Brothers' New York theater. With the popularization of jazz during the 1920s, the cooch became the "shimmy," an even more explicitly sexual performance.

The United States long maintained (and for many still does) a dualistic, almost schizophrenic, moral standard when it comes to nighttime

Sophie Tucker, Stage singer (SAYRE 10136). *Wikimedia Commons.*

pleasures. At the birth of the twentieth century, the country's official moral standard adhered to Victorian virtues: Americans were to be reserved and virtuous; sex was accepted for procreation but not for erotic pleasure; women were expected to be passive and accommodating; and entertainment was formal, chaperoned, suggestive but not erotic. Socially worthy men and, most especially, women were expected to live wholesome lives, particularly when they socialized together. However, a popular wink-and-a-nod civic custom accepted red-light districts as a necessary evil in which low-life sexual degenerates, racial minorities and wayward upper-crust males were permitted to fulfill unspeakable desires. The decades between 1890 and 1930 witnessed the erosion of the lines separating these spheres of moral life.

Sophie Tucker's career spans the tumultuous period in which New York—and American—nightlife was remade. Born Sophie Kalishin in 1884, while her mother was in transit from Russia to America, she grew up in Hartford, Connecticut, where the family took the name Abusa (sometimes called Abuza) and ran a kosher restaurant. From an early age, Tucker resisted the traditional patriarchal dictates of Orthodox Judaism, family life and the thankless work at the Abusa Home Restaurant. In rebellion at age sixteen, "fat and unhappy," she married a neighbor, Louis Tuck, only to realize shortly thereafter that it was a mistake. Pregnant, she returned home and gave birth to her only child, Burt, in 1906.

"After the baby's birth, with a sense of entrapment growing," Erenberg reports, Sophie left her son with her parents, an almost unheard-of act for the period, and "made her break to New York and show business."[93] She got her first flush of the entertainment experience singing as a teenager in amateur programs held in Hartford fairs and parks, often identified as the "the fat girl." Coming to Gotham, Sophie Kalish/Abusa-Tuck renamed herself Tucker and joined a growing chorus of ethnic immigrants remaking popular entertainment. Other Jewish immigrant talent included Al Jolson and Eddie Cantor; Irish performers like Guinan and Morton Downey; Italian entertainers like Jimmy Durante; the Polish star, Gilda Gray; and a growing number of African American artists like James Reese Europe, Bert Williams and Bill "Bojangles" Robinson.

Tucker's professional career began in 1908, and over the next two decades, she repositioned her stage presence from a burlesque "shouter" to a vaudeville performer to a cabaret personality to a speakeasy hostess. She began her career, like Al Jolson and Bert Williams, in blackface. In 1908, one of her first gigs in New York was with a burlesque troupe with which she gained notoriety as a "coon shouter." Blackface minstrelsy was a popular form of entertainment during the late nineteenth century that died out during the 1920s. Blackface was makeup worn by both White and Black entertainers that confirmed racism while subverting it. Blackface depicted fictitious myths about African Americans that were meant to vindicate White privilege but also confirm myths that subverted the fiction of such privilege, especially around notions of sexuality, "primitivism" and authenticity—qualities denied repressed upper-class Protestant White people. Equally critical, early-twentieth-century sexism, much like today, forced female entertainers to choose between performing as a more repressed starlet or a shouter, as sexy or outrageous; Tucker, like Bessie Smith, Guinan, Mae West, Madonna, Lady Gaga and other female entertainers who followed them turned the shouter into a cultural icon.

Tucker's evolving representation exemplified the transformation of the nightlife stage. Performance evolved from something formal, distant from the audience, to an informal environment in which the patron shared in the evening's pleasures with the performer. Tucker achieved celebrity during a period in which the line between the performer and the patron broke down. She helped make nightlife entertainment a closer, more intimate partygoing experience. The dance floor replaced the classical proscenium arch, the spotlight replaced the footlight and the onstage band replaced musicians in the pit. Where once the star spoke down from the stage to her audience, Tucker and other entertainers established an eye-level relation with their fans, connecting directly with the club's customers. Where she once wore blackface, now heavy theatrical makeup was removed and the performer appeared more natural, more real. The female performer warmly welcomed patrons into an informal venue with cramped table seating, smaller meals, loud music and a popular dance floor. She celebrated a vital cabaret culture that promoted a new public intimacy of sociability, inebriation and sexuality.

In 1925, and at the height of Prohibition, Tucker opened her own nightclub, Playground. More than a decade earlier, she had originated the role of the host that defined the modern nightspot. Now, the queen of the cabaret was competing with Guinan, Morgan and others for the title Queen of the Speakeasy. It was a title she would not capture.

Most speakeasy hostesses were far less glamorous than Guinan, Tucker, Morgan and other upscale sisters. But not unlike Tex, their job was to encourage men to spend money. Sexual-tinged familiarity was one way to help separate the male patron from his cash. These hostesses, and many of the showgirls at the clubs, allowed men to kiss and fondle them, while some sat on a customer's lap or allowed them to rub their legs. In distinction from taxi-hall dancers, speakeasy hostesses and dancers normally did not touch a male patron's genitals or engage in sex acts with patrons. However, because of their low pay and other factors, some hostesses did turn to prostitution.

A Bathtub Mystery

Prohibition reached its zenith at a 1926 Washington's Birthday party given by Broadway impresario Earl Carroll. His "Vanities" show competed with Florence Ziegfeld's "Follies" and George White's "Scandals." Each relied on skimpily dressed chorus girls to draw an audience. On Monday, February 22, Carroll organized a special post-show event that drew an estimated two to five hundred of New York's well-to-do. An exchange between Broadway personalities George S. Kaufman and Groucho Marx suggests the Follies' appeal:

> *Kaufman: "What do you think of Earl Carroll's 'Vanities'?"*
> *Marx: "I had rather not say. I saw it under bad conditions—the curtain was up."*[94]

The party's centerpiece was a special performance by a young starlet, the seventeen-year-old chorine Joyce Hawley. At the end of the regularly scheduled show, Carroll invited the guests to stay on for a special treat. The Vanities' showgirls, dressed in negligees and bathing suits, paraded among the patrons, offering cocktails and ginger ale. As the evening wore on, celebrities showed up, including Harry Thaw, who killed the celebrated architect Stanford White in 1906; Countess Vera Cathcart, self-promoting adulteress; and Philip A. Payne, editor of the *Daily Mirror*. Guests were invited to participate in a Charleston contest and judge a bathing beauty contest among the Vanities' showgirls.

Behind the stage's curtain, Carroll had set up a special bathtub. How it operated and what it was filled with remain mysteries to this day. Some say the bathtub's spigot was connected to a hose that fed a special beverage. Some insisted that the liquid was only ginger ale, while others who sampled the liquid insisted it was champagne. Nevertheless, a surprise awaited those in attendance.

At about 4:00 a.m., the bathtub was brought out from behind the curtain, and Carroll appeared with Hawley dressed only in a modest chemise and shoes. Carroll held up a cloak, allowing Hawley to disrobe and step into the bathtub. After she settled in, he dropped the cloak and, with glass in hand, welcomed the audience: "Gentlemen, the line forms on the left." A dozen or so partygoers quickly lined up to dip their glasses for a sample of the unique concoction. According to some accounts, Hawley was not prepared for such a public spectacle and burst into tears. After she fled in shame, the party petered out and the patrons went off to other haunts for still other late-night indulgences.

Over the next few days, press reports about the party became front-page headlines, and outrage among moralists mounted. Something had to be done! Hurriedly, a federal grand jury called Carroll to testify over whether alcohol was served and whether a nude woman performed. He insisted that neither took place. On the first issue, the prosecutor could not substantiate the charge. However, after Hawley testified about her performance and that Carroll refused to pay her the promised $1,000 fee, he was found guilty of perjury. He was fined $2,000 and sentenced to a federal penitentiary for a year and a day.

5
PARTY TIME DOWNTOWN

As the irony of city life dictates, Texas Guinan lived in Greenwich Village but was never really a part of the Village scene. Reflecting on her life in the Village, she said, "Some great artists struggle in my neighborhood. They live in studios and there are other artists who want to prove their greatness by drawing—on their friends." With her usual wit, she noted, "The Streets are crooked and the people's ideas match the streets."[95]

Throughout all her years in New York, she lived near Washington Square Park but remained a Broadway woman, drawn by its big drinks, big shows and big spenders. She was not attracted to the ethnic, working-class people, particularly Italian, Irish and African Americans, who had long made the Village their home, nor to the counterculture then reshaping the Village from an ethnic neighborhood to a bohemian mecca.

During the first century and a half of New York's development, the Village was a secluded suburb and farming area. Following the American Revolution, the city purchased what is today's Washington Square Park to establish a potter's field and public gallows. It was only after a series of yellow fever and cholera outbreaks beset the city at the end of the eighteenth and beginning of nineteenth centuries that a significant northward migration began to remake the Village.

By the early twentieth century, the Village had taken on the quaint, heterogeneous character that still defines it. It was marked by low-scale, Federal-style, single-family housing; extensive less-valued properties that encouraged affordable apartment buildings and overcrowding; and narrow,

Washington Square Arch.
Wikimedia Commons.

crooked, non-grid, tree-lined streets better suited for horse-and-carriage transport than modern automobile traffic. This encouraged the settlement of a diverse population made up of well-to-do strivers and professionals, blue-collar wage workers, immigrant and ethnic communities and a diverse assortment of bohemian artists and writers.

The cultural life of the Village underwent its first transformation in 1912, when Mabel Dodge organized evenings at her apartment at 23 5th Avenue, just north of Washington Square Park's famed arch. One night, the still young Carl Van Vechten attended. He met Dodge while making his first grand tour of Europe, visiting her palatial villa in Florence. She moved back to New York in 1912 with her son, leaving her second husband behind, and plunged into the city's rapidly growing upper-crust bohemian scene. Dodge's Evenings served as an intellectual incubator for a remarkably diverse group of artists, writers, political activists and even psychiatrists to critically engage the major issues of the day. Among the luminaries who regularly assembled at the salon were writers Lincoln Steffens, Amy Lowell and Thornton Wilder; activists Margaret Sanger, Emma Goldman, John Reed, "Big Bill" Haywood and Roger Baldwin; dancer Isadora Duncan; and A.A. Brill, Freud's principal disciple in America. As Stanley Walker,

Portrait of Mabel Dodge Luhan by Carl Van Vechten. *Library of Congress, Control Number 2004663225.*

the grand chronicler of Gotham life, reminds us, "For each generation, according to its own romantic or intellectual inclinations, creates a Village somewhat in its own image."[96]

One night, Van Vechten invited two African American entertainers to perform at Dodge's salon. A historian described their performance as follows: "A woman in high-button boots and white stockings danced a jig while her male partner sang a popular song and strummed a banjo."[97] The performance upset Dodge. "While an appalling Negress danced before us in white stockings and buttoned shoes, the man strummed a banjo and sang an embarrassing song," she bemoaned. "They both leered and rolled their suggestive eyes and made me feel first hot and then cold, for I had never been so near this kind of thing before; but Carl rocked with laughter and little shrieks escaped him as he clapped his pretty hands."[98]

For better or worse, as Andrea Barnet reminds us, "Dodge's salon was where black Harlem first met Greenwich Village bohemia and, conversely, where white bohemia got its first taste of a parallel black culture that it would soon not only glorify but actively try to emulate."[99] Helping create the right atmosphere, Dodge's attentive butler, Vittorio, whom she had brought from Florence, graciously offered Pinch scotch and Gorgonzola cheese and ham sandwiches.

SPEAKEASY VILLAGE

By the time of the First World War, the Village was in full swing. The 1919 Bolshevik Revolution in Russia sparked a Red Scare in the United States, characterized by an aggressive campaign against anarchists, communists, socialists and other dissidents. New York was at the center of this campaign, especially the Lower East Side with its immigrant radicals and the Village with its free thinkers. However, once the bloodletting—with its roundups, trials, imprisonments and deportations of thousands of alleged radicals—ran its course by the early 1920s, the scare died down.

Against this background, a bold bohemian culture blossomed. The poets Wallace Stevens and Edna St. Vincent Millay, the playwright Eugene O'Neill, the novelists Sinclair Lewis and Floyd Dell, the critic Edmund Wilson and the photographer Berenice Abbott, among many others, arrived in the Village before the war and helped pollinate the new atmosphere. During the Roaring Twenties, their collective artistry became the voice and vision of the nation. This artistry embraced both creative and sexual freedom, making the Village—as was the case in Harlem—a popular haven for gay men and women. F. Scott Fitzgerald caught the spirit of period in his most memorable work, the 1925 classic *The Great Gatsby*. It is but a thinly veiled

In-home still—NYPD 9159 photo of still at 163 Attorney Street, July 19, 1927. *Det. Gilligan, NYPD Collection, NYC Municipal Archives.*

report of what he and Zelda experienced in the alcohol-induced swirl of high-society life during Prohibition.

The Village's celebrated "free love" culture of the prewar era provided the soil for the flowering of a vital homosexual community during Prohibition. Among the dozens of speaks catering to a predominate gay and lesbian clientele were the Flower Pot, run by Dolly Judge at the corner of Christopher and Gay Streets; the Red Mask, run by Jackie Mason on Charles Street; and Paul and Joe's, located at 6th Avenue at 9th Street (it eventually moved to 19th Street to escape police crackdowns). The most popular featured drag queens like Jackie Law. A new sexual tolerance between gay and straight men marked many of these clubs. As historian George Chauncey points out, "Queer and straight men thus thought themselves as sexually incompatible as well as sexually different."[100]

The Village became a center for speakeasy culture because of its reputation as a tolerant bohemian district and the presence of local residents, who, for ethnic and political reasons, rejected the imposition of Prohibition. Ruth Wittenberg, a longtime Village civic activist, recalled the resistance to Prohibition. "People went to places, and my house was one of them, where you could always find a drink," she noted. "And it wasn't always bathtub gin. It was good liquor that somebody smuggled in somehow." The diversity of the Village populace set the stage for a complex, variegated speakeasy culture—one that changed throughout the '20s. As Walker reminds us, "The Village, true to its reputation as a hell-hole, probably was the easiest place in New York to get a drink."[101]

Restaurants remained the principal venues for the consumption of liquor with meals. They often served locally produced wine and were popular among Italians. Wittenberg vividly recalled the restaurant scene during the '20s. "Practically every restaurant was a speakeasy. The good restaurants all had liquor, and the police raids were infrequent. There was more liquor than there had been before Prohibition." She added, they "operat[ed] more or less secretly behind locked doors or wide open with liquor sales limited to known patrons."

Caroline Ware, in her classic sociological study *Greenwich Village, 1920–1930*, provides the most in-depth analysis of Prohibition's influence on Village life. She identifies a half-dozen different types of speakeasies that operated throughout the Village, each providing a distinct atmosphere and attracting a different clientele. Some old-time saloons survived after the imposition of Prohibition. Run by Village locals, these watering holes operated predominately within the Irish community, tended to have an almost exclusive male clientele and, not surprising, remained tied to old-fashioned Tammany Hall politics.

Restaurants remained the principal venues for the consumption of liquor with meals. As Ware found, they "operat[ed] more or less secretly behind locked doors or wide open with liquor sales limited to known patrons."[102] She also points out that by 1930, restaurants were the most numerous and highly competitive speakeasies. At bars, like older saloons, "liquor was cut, prices high, women usually admitted and prominent, and location less conspicuous." They tended to draw non-Village partygoers, including college-aged and single people. The cordial shop, an innovative speak, emerged in the late 1920s. Ware identifies them as "fly-by-night affairs, renting a store on Friday, setting carpenters to works and being ready for business on Saturday night, here today and gone tomorrow." Ware also estimates that 40 tearooms operated in the Village during the '20s by locals "who identified with their patrons." She points out, "The tea rooms really belonged to the bohemian stage of the Village and the proprietors were capitalizing essentially on the spirit of bohemia."[103]

Finally, cabarets served nonresidents, drawn by the Village's exotic reputation. They emerged at the end of World War I and offered "relatively low-prices and were patronized more by college boys and girls out for a good time than were the midtown night clubs." Some were "'pick-up joints,' others 'served good dollar dinners" and another "had a Lesbian reputation." Ware points out that they "sold 'atmosphere' rather than the glitter and nudity which brought high profits to midtown night clubs."

Ware also notes that different types of speakeasies tended to dominate the Village during each of the three phases of Prohibition. For example, during the pre-Prohibition period, the "old fashion corner saloons, like Irish 'gin mills'" and German beer gardens were the principal watering holes. However, this changed as Prohibition took effect. Ware points out that "the post-Prohibition liquor industry was a new business with new people, new methods, and a new clientele." She says that in the early phase of Prohibition, tearooms brought outsiders to the Village for "amusement and excitement." She describes these speaks as "dingy, 'hole-in-wall' places, stowed away with utmost secrecy and entered only with knock and password by those who were known." Alcohol cost forty dollars a gallon, gin five dollars or more a quart. She found that during the mid-years of Prohibition, the cabaret was prominent and notes that Italians in the Village not only made wine but also began to sell it commercially, especially through local restaurants and groceries.

During Prohibition's late period, smaller, dedicated speakeasies dominated, with many Village residents working as bootleggers. By 1930, the atmosphere had profoundly changed: speaks had their "steady and eminently respectable customers—local and non-local Irish, new residents, politicians, teachers, professional and business people." Liquor was regularly tested before being sold; the sale of liquor became extensive and reputable. As Ware points out, "Every sort of store—grocer, cigar store, barber shop, bootblack, etc.—sold some form of the prohibited beverage. Police estimated that by 1930, that there were thousands of places in and around the Village selling liquor."[104]

Barney's Playground

If midtown had Texas Guinan and Harlem had Edwin Smalls, then the Village had Barney Gallant. Walker describes him as "of medium height. His hair is black, turning grey, and it sticks up above an oval face with black eyes....He dresses with great care. He speaks rapidly and sharply. He doesn't smoke, but he will drink anything in reason." He had but one guiding principle: "Every man should be his own Jesus."[105] Gallant gained renown as the first person to go to jail for violating Prohibition laws.

Gallant entered the speakeasy business in 1919, when he, along with Frank Conroy, Hal Meltzer and Margaret Barker purchased the Greenwich Village Inn after the death of its owner, George Barker. However, in October

1919, the police raided the Inn, and Gallant was charged with illegally selling alcohol. Appearing before Judge Learned Hand, he pleaded guilty and received a thirty-day prison sentence.

Gallant was a Russian-Jewish immigrant who arrived in Baltimore with his parents in 1903. He moved to St. Louis as a youth and got a cub reporter job at the *Post-Dispatch*. In 1909, he relocated to New York, settled in the Village and stayed with Eugene O'Neill in a one-room cold-water apartment with no electricity on West 4th Street. During the prewar period, he socialized with the bohemian crowd remaking the Village, including Millay, the Barrymores and Theodore Dreiser.

Recovering from his first venture into club life, Gallant opened his second speak, Club Gallant, at 40 Washington Square South, in December 1921. Barney's good friend Noël Coward often contributed skits, which Gallant never used. As Walker found, "It was the easily the swankiest place in the Village—no place for a starving artist to pass the evening, but perfect for those who had money." Among club regulars were performers from the Greenwich Village Follies, a musical revue created by John Murray Anderson that originated at the Greenwich Village Theater near Sheridan Square. Drink prices were steep: a bottle of scotch cost sixteen dollars and a bottle of champagne was twenty-five.

Barney catered to high-end partygoers, as did Guinan and other upscale club promoters. "Exclusiveness is the night club's great and only stock in trade," he argued. "Take this away and the glamour and romance and mystery are gone. The night club manager realizes that he must pander to the hidden and unconscious snobbery of the great majorities. It is because they make it so difficult to access that everybody is fighting to get into them."

In 1925, Gallant moved to a third club, at 85 West 3rd Street, and it ran for six years. He always retained and catered to a high-class clientele. By January 1932, he again moved his club, this time to 19 Washington Square North, the scene of a shocking murder, and rechristened it the Washington Square Club. In keeping with his management philosophy, only those known to Barney or his doorman were allowed entry. It had a large dance floor and a five-piece band; maintained a splendid circular bar; offered excellent French cuisine; and could comfortably accommodate 120 patrons. As Walker found, "It was a success in spite of the depression." Gallant is most remembered for the cocktail he invented, the Lipstick. This unique concoction called for two parts champagne, one part gin, one part orange juice, a dash of grapefruit juice and a trickle of cherry brandy. It was promoted as "sweet but with a wallop."

Eva Kotchever "Eve Addams" on right with an unidentified woman. *Wikimedia Commons.*

During Prohibition, Greenwich Village flowered as a vital homosexual mecca. MacDougal Street, just south of Washington Square, was the epicenter of the gay scene, perfect for cruising, with popular restaurants, cafés and, of course, speaks. Among the dozens of clubs catering to a predominate gay and lesbian clientele were the Flower Pot, run by Dolly Judge at the corner of Christopher and Gay Streets and the Red Mask, run by Jackie Mason on Charles Street. Still other clubs included the Black Rabbit at MacDougal Street and Minetta Lane; Louis' Luncheon at 116 MacDougal Street; Julian's at 159 West 10th Street; and the Bungalow.

Perhaps the most notorious lesbian gathering place was Eve's Place (aka Hangout and Tearoom) at 129 MacDougal Street. Between 1925 and '26, Eve Addams (aka Eva Kotchever), a Polish Jewish lesbian émigré, ran a popular after-theater club. In the spirit of the '20s, Addams hosted regular salons featuring poetry readings, musical performances and discussion of popular topics, including sex. Chauncey found that it displayed a provocative sign on the door: "Men are admitted but not welcome."

Some of Addams's neighbors considered her "the queen of the third sex," while others, sadly, condemned her as a "man-hater" and for hosting a club "where ladies prefer each other." She was busted by an undercover female cop in the summer of '27 who engaged her a conversation about lesbian love. Addams showed the cop her unpublished short story collection, *Lesbian Love*; she was convicted of disorderly conduct and obscenity and deported. Nevertheless, in 1931, a Village columnist fondly recalled Addams's club as "one of the most delightful hang-outs the Village ever had."[106] The Village offered still other entertainment. Paul and Joe's, originally located at 6th Avenue at 9th Street, was the most popular pansy club, featuring drag queens like Jackie Law. In addition, the Liberal Club hosted regular drag balls at Webster Hall on East 11th Street.

6
PARTY TIME UPTOWN

Swingin'

Texas Guinan regularly ventured uptown to Harlem, as did the rich and famous, where they rarely rubbed shoulders with local bootleggers and gamblers, maids and deliverymen. The celebrity crowd ranged from to Jack Dempsey and Joan Crawford to Bix Beiderbecke, Paul Whiteman, Hoagy Carmichael, Mae West, Helen Morgan, Tallulah Bankhead, Beatrice Lillie, Benny Goodman and Gene Tunney. The notorious lesbian cross-dresser Gladys Bentley and her raunchy sidekick, Jackie (famously known as "Moms") Mabley, were never excluded.

Everyone showed up at Pod's and Jerry's, aka the Catagonia Club, a speak at 133rd Street between 7th and Lennox Avenues. Willie "The Lion" Smith, the club's legendary pianist, claimed "customers…varied from tush hogs to the biggest names on Broadway." The club was run by Jerry Preston, a local gambler, and Charles Hollingsworth, affectionately known as Pod because he greeted patrons with a welcoming, "Howdy, *pod*-ner!" It was celebrated for its great jazz, affordable prices (drinks cost one dollar) and being Harlem's most integrated nightspot. It was, along with the Ebony Club and Smalls Paradise, one of the notable exceptions to nearly all wet zone and uptown speakeasies that barred Black and White patrons from being seated at the same tables, let alone next to each other. At Pod's and Jerry's, if White guests objected to sitting with Black patrons, they were asked to leave.[107]

Portrait of Willie Smith in his apartment, Manhattan, New York (January 1947), William P. Gottlieb. *Library of Congress Music Division, Digital ID gottlieb 07921.*

Also, like many uptown hideaways, at Pod and Jerry's, drink flowed as freely as marijuana. At one point during the late 1920s, Preston jazzed up the building's décor and officially named it the Log Cabin. Everyone still called it Pod's and Jerry's.

The speak's informal, racially mixed atmosphere combined with great music kept patrons coming back for more. Smith, born Henry Joseph Bonaparte Bertholf, was one of Ellington's mentors and the big draw. He revolutionized popular music by introducing the stride piano and was among jazz's first solo pianists. In Newark, New Jersey, Smith's mother was a cleaning woman to a Jewish family, and along with the family's children, Smith received a Jewish education, learning Hebrew. He was bar mitzvahed and converted to Judaism. Smith got his nickname during the Great War, serving in an all-Black U.S. Army unit in France as an artillery gunner; as legend has it, an officer commented, "Smith, you're a lion with that gun."

A young Black woman and recent transplant to Harlem from Baltimore wandered into Pod's and Jerry's looking for a singing gig toward the tail end of Prohibition. She had performed at other Harlem haunts but wanted something more regular. Preston offered her two dollars a night, plus tips, and she gladly accepted. After an awkward adjustment to Smith's style, the young singer found her footing and began one of the most celebrated careers in American music. The performer was Billie Holiday.

Portrait of Billie Holiday, *Downbeat*, New York, (circa February 1947), William P. Gottlieb. *Library of Congress Prints and Photographs Division, Reproduction Number LC-GLB23-0425 DLC.*

THE UPTOWN SCENE

Harlem became the Black mecca during the Roaring Twenties. Its development was fueled in part by what is known as the Great Migration, the massive exodus of poor Black (and some White) people from the rural South to cities of the North in the East and Midwest during the waning days of the 1800s. It was a migration spurred as much by the promise of economic opportunity as by a desire to flee post-Reconstruction or Jim Crow racism and southern poverty. As Gilbert Osofsky bitterly points out in his classic study *Harlem: The Making of a Ghetto*, "There were more Negroes lynched, burned, tortured and disenfranchised in the late eighties, nineties and the first decade of the twentieth century than any other time in our history."[108] This migration remade Chicago, Detroit and, most importantly, Gotham.

African Americans have been a part of New York since it was still New Amsterdam; in 1626, only two years after the city's formal settlement, the Dutch West India Company unloaded eleven African slaves. Over the following three centuries, as Osofsky reminds us, "At no period in the history of New York City were Negroes accepted as full American citizens."[109] Black New Yorkers lived in squalid neighborhood pockets amid other poor ethnic (and often immigrant) groups. With each generation, African Americans steadily relocated uptown as Manhattan kept pushing northward. Between the Revolution and Civil War, they clustered in what was known as the Five Points or "Stagg Town" in today's Chinatown. Following the Civil War and its horrendous 1863 Draft Riot, Black New Yorkers relocated to "Little Africa" in the West Village. Over the subsequent decades, Black residents were pushed farther uptown on the west side to the Tenderloin (23rd to 42nd Streets), then San Juan Hill (59th to 65th Streets) until they finally reached Harlem.

Three unrelated developments helped remake Harlem, setting the stage for the formation of the Black mecca. First, the Great Migration (and immigration from the Caribbean) radically increased the African American population in New York. Second, the old-world village of Harlem, long known as the city's first suburb, went through a speculative housing development boom and bust. The White gentry who were expected to fill the new apartment buildings and townhouses never arrived, leaving a significant glut in the housing stock. Third, the city extended the subway system uptown into Harlem, thus providing affordable transportation farther north.

Between 1900 and 1930, the Black population of New York exploded fivefold. In the short-lived recession that occurred in the wake of World War I, Harlem was filled with many empty apartments. Enterprising Black real estate agents welcomed both the older, established leaders of the Black bourgeoisie and the young turks of the new cultural movement setting the stage for the flowering of the Harlem Renaissance. The old guard consisted of such legendary figures as W.E.B. DuBois, James Weldon Johnson and Marcus Garvey. The "new blood" included writers like Langston Hughes, Wallace Thurman, Zora Neale Hurston and Claude McKay.

Well-heeled White "slummers" were attracted to Harlem in the '20s as much by the presence of alcohol and other vices as the seductive appeal of the historically "foreign" African American. "In the twenties, the ludicrous image of the Negro as 'darky' became a subordinate theme," Osofsky notes, "eclipsed by the conception of the Negro as sensuous and rhythmic African."[110] The old antebellum slave, celebrated in song and blackface, began to give way to a truer, more complex, African American identity. Downtown White society looked at the uptown Harlem scene, and the artists and musicians, men and women, who symbolized it, as a bridge to the primitive, a stepping-stone to the natural world, closer, truer to Freud's unrepressed id. Unfortunately, White "appreciation" for the primitive contained its own negation: If African Americans were those most resistant to modern society, they were then most unsuited for a "normal" middle-class life—the "respectable" middle-class life consisting of marriage, children, home and, for the male, a successful career depending on conformity to corporate order. Being primitive made being normal impossible.

The primitivism represented by the African American was a social fiction that was both articulated and resisted by many artists within what was known as the New Negroes of the Harlem Renaissance. This generation of artists and thinkers, scholars and musicians, journalists and poets, writers and painters vividly articulated the 1920s mounting crisis of capitalism. The stage of mercantile capitalism, with its attendant mass industrialization and colonial imperialism, was reaching its zenith. The requirement of mass manufacturing and a global market challenged the old-world order. A new world was being established, one that integrated primitive, psychophysical resistance into the cycle of capitalist consumerism. As Walker witnessed, "The invasion by the whites of the Harlem clubs, in particular, created a situation which could have caused serious trouble. It didn't."[111]

Party Time, Uptown

New York uptown nightlife embodied a particular form of northern racism. Harlem speaks were famous for their invocation of the primitive, for their jazz, Black entertainers, free-flowing alcohol and other illegal pleasures. In most of the upscale nightspots, African Americans could entertain and serve White clientele but were barred from club management and as patrons. This factor shaped Harlem's speakeasy scene, creating in effect three tiers of uptown nightlife. The first tier consisted of the high-end speaks like the Cotton Club that catered to a nearly all-White clientele and featured spectacular Black revues. The second tier was made up of nightclubs like Pod's and Jerry's that catered to a mixed but often predominantly African American clientele and offered popular entertainment. Finally, a third tier consisted of the innumerable, and essentially Black-only, speaks like the Sugar Cane Club that pushed the limits of acceptable morals. All featured illegal alcohol.

Party time uptown didn't get started until after midnight. The center of Harlem nightlife, West 133rd Street between Lenox and 7th Avenues, was known as Jungle Alley and hosted a half-dozen popular speaks. As Billie Holiday recalled, "133rd Street was the real swing street…like 52nd Street later tried to be." West 52nd Street emerged in the wake of the Depression and Harlem riots of 1935 that drove the jazz scene, and White patrons, downtown; it flourished well into the 1980s. E. Simms Campbell's famous 1932 map of Harlem, *A Night-Club Map of Harlem*, conveys much of the excitement, if not the actual geography, of the uptown scene.

The Cotton Club was the most famous Harlem nightspot and the capstone of first-tier speakeasy culture. It has been immortalized in movies, music and literature; a club bearing its name still operates on 125th Street. Duke Ellington recalled the original club as "a classy spot." The unofficial story has it that the gangster Owney Madden took it over following his release from

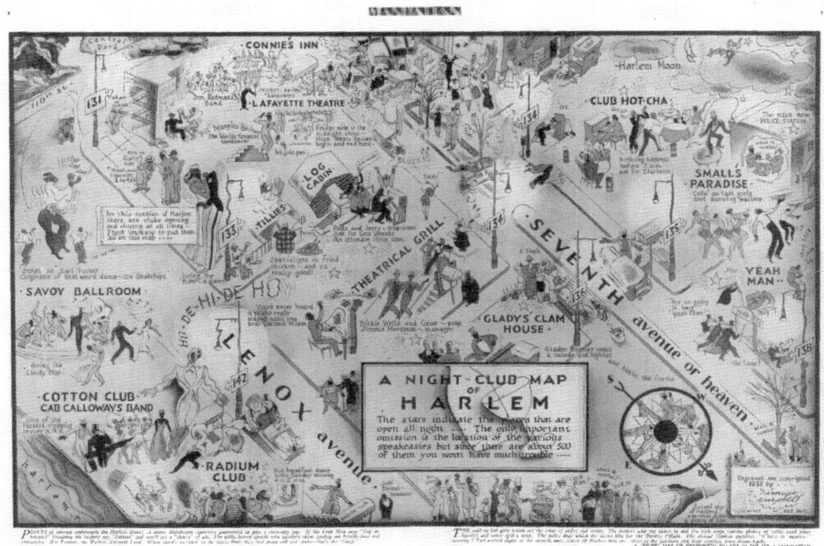

"A night-club map of Harlem," E. Simms (Elmer Simms) Campbell (1933). *Library of Congress Control Number 2016585261.*

Above: The Cotton Club, 142nd Street and Lenox Avenue. *Wikimedia Commons.*

Right: Duke Ellington directing his band from the piano at the Hurricane Ballroom, New York, April 1943. *Library of Congress Prints & Photographs Online Catalog (PPOC), Farm Security Administration–Office of War Information Photograph Collection, Digital ID fsa 8d13224.*

Sing Sing penitentiary in 1923. The club was located on the second floor of the former Douglas Casino (which became the Golden Gate Ballroom) at the corner of 142nd Street and Lenox Avenue. During pre-Prohibition days, Jack Johnson, the former heavyweight boxing champ, ran it as the Club De Luxe, a cabaret seating four hundred people. Madden refashioned it into an upscale nightspot and backed it during its glory days.

The Cotton Club was designed by the noted architect Joseph Urban and featured a large, horseshoe-shaped ballroom with a raised dance floor and bandstand. It seated seven hundred patrons along two tiers of crowded but well-appointed tables that ringed the performance area. Ironically, it used artificial palm trees to create an antebellum plantation-like setting, one that only exaggerated the Jim Crow racism separating the club's patrons from the wait staff and performers. This upscale speak was renowned for its chorus line of twelve dancing girls and eight showgirls who, according to Ellington, "were all beautiful." The female dancers were "high yeller" or had a near-white complexion, all under twenty-one years of age and over five feet, six inches in height. The legendary Lena Horne got her start on its chorus line when she was only sixteen years old.

Between 1927 and 1931, Ellington and his band, the Washingtonians, were the Cotton Club's featured attraction. Many notable Black entertainers, as well as mixed-raced groups, including one with Carl Van Vechten, the White publicist of Harlem nightlife, were refused admission. However, after establishing himself, Ellington was able to secure a small table near the kitchen for special Black guests. "During the Prohibition period," he recalled, "you could always buy good whiskey from somebody at the Cotton Club."[112] However, the speak had a special deal: "They use to have what they call Chicken Cock. It was in a bottle in a can, and the can was sealed. It cost something like ten to fourteen dollars a pint. That was when I use to drink whisky as though it were water." He further remembered, "Sunday night in the Cotton Club was the night. All the big New York stars in town, no matter where they were playing, showed up at the Cotton Club to take bows....The performers were paid high salaries, and prices for customers were high too."

Lena Horne by William P. Gottlieb, between 1946 and 1948. *Library of Congress, LC Classification LC-GLB23- 0429.*

Barney Josephson, owner of Café Society, a legendary West Village nightspot the operated from 1938 to '48 in Sheridan Square, was a White man who regularly made it to the Cotton Club. "The booze was all bootleg," he recalled. "In those days you could bring your bottle. You bought your own pint on your hip, and they would serve you a glass bucket of ice cubes and splits of ginger ale or soda water, just one little bottle, enough to make one highball, and they would charge you a good price on it. They made as much on that shit as they did on whiskey."[113]

One of the Cotton Club's major competitors was Connie's Inn, a speak operated by George and Connie Immerman at 7th Avenue and 131st Street. It was popular because it regularly showcased cabaret revues, including *Ain't Misbehavin'*. It normally prohibited Black patrons but made an exception for the queen of the uptown party scene, A'Lelia Walker, daughter of the first African American female millionaire, Madame C.J. Walker. She considered Connie's her favorite nightspot. However, the *New York Age*, a leading Black paper, charged the Immerman brothers with pushing the worst hooch in Harlem and for barring less well-to-do Black patrons but permitting "'slummers,' sports, 'coke addicts,' and high rollers of the white race who came to Harlem to indulge in illicit and illegal recreation."[114]

Barron D. Wilkins, a legendary Harlem gangster, businessman and political figure, operated another upscale and essentially Qhite speak, the Exclusive Club, at 198 West 134th Street at 7th Avenue. A fierce African

Left: Stage production of *Hot Chocolates* as seen from audience at Connie's Inn, Harlem, New York City, circa 1920. *New York Public Library, Schomburg Center for Research in Black Culture, Catalog ID b14907056.*

Below: Smalls' Paradise postcard. *Wikimedia Commons.*

SMALL'S PARADISE. 135th STREET and 7th AVE., NEW YORK CITY

American entrepreneur, he opened his first speak in the Tenderloin during the prewar era and operated it under different names before settling into its most famous moniker, the Exclusive. Its atmosphere was, as Walker noted, "where the songs were, to be blunt about it, filthy."[115] Wilkins was a big, gregarious man who had a special affinity for Black athletes like Jack Johnson, whom he helped finance his world heavyweight championship run. Yellow Charleston, an uptown gambler and whiskey supplier, stabbed Barron to death near his club in 1926.

Moving up 7th Avenue to 135th Street, one found Smalls Paradise, an upscale speak operated by Edwin Smalls that was open to Black and White patrons. It was famous for its big-band jam sessions, colorful floor shows and waiters "who danced the Charleston while balancing full trays on their

View of the Savoy Ballroom at night, on Lenox Avenue between 140th and 141st Streets, in Harlem, circa 1950. *New York Public Library, Schomburg Center for Research in Black Culture, Catalog ID b12017637*

fingertips." According to the knowledgeable Jervis Anderson, it was "the most accessible to ordinary Harlemites. Not many of them could afford its prices, but those who could were more welcome there than they were at the other top places."[116] On weekends, Smalls was so popular that a reservation was required.

A different evening's entertainment took place at the Savoy Ballroom, located on Lenox Avenue between 140th and 141st Streets. It was a dance palace that drew more than four thousand partygoers for its opening night bash in March 1926. Upon entering this cathedral of hot entertainment, patrons ascended two flights of marble steps with, like a palace of old, mirrors running along the adjourning walls. At the second floor, partygoers entered a large dance hall running 50 feet wide by 250 feet long and featuring a burnished maple floorboard. A shiny brass rail ran along the perimeter and a raised bandstand anchored the evening's entertainment. Various warm-up acts performed until 1:30 a.m. when Fletcher Henderson and his Rainbow Orchestra made its triumphant appearance.

During the '20s Harlem roared, especially at the Savoy. In addition to Henderson and his band, the dance palace welcomed all the top big-band jazz leaders, including Ellington, Louis Armstrong, Cab Calloway, King Oliver and Chick Webb. Every night at the Savoy was a special night. Tuesday night was the '20's equivalent to today's *American Idol* with, at an event called the 400 Club, serious dancers jammed all night. And the most popular dance of the period, the Lindy hop, was named after a true high flyer, Charles Lindbergh. On Thursday night, the night maids had off, the club hosted the Kitchen Mechanics' Night, slang for maids and cooks. Saturday was disparaged as Square's Night, a night popular among downtown slummers or, even more disparagingly, Whites into cabareting. Sunday night at the Savoy was the most glamorous, attracting famous social worthies, movie stars and other celebrities.

ANOTHER UPTOWN

The Sugar Cane Club was a late-night uptown speak, off-limits to the casual White slummer. Operated by Edwin Smalls, the impresario of the legendary Smalls Paradise, the Sugar Cane was located on 135th Street and 5th Avenue. Roi Ottley, a noted African American author, journalist and acute observer of Harlem nightlife, knew the club well: "It was a damp, dimly lit cellar, with two-dozen tables surrounding a tiny dance floor."[117] Popularly known as the Cat on the Saxophone, the poet laureate of the Harlem Renaissance, Langston Hughes, celebrated the club in his first published collection, *The Weary Blues*.[118]

EVERYBODY
Half-pint,
Gin?
No, make it
LOVES MY BABY
corn. You like
liquor,
don't you honey?
BUT MY BABY
Sure. Kiss me,
DON'T LOVE NOBODY
daddy.
BUT ME.

This speak was not fancy. Located in a basement, it measured only 25 by 125 feet and was marked by an earthy smell. The entrance was guarded by a man seated behind the front window, who, if he knew the visitor, pulled a long chain connected to a bolt on the entrance door that let the customer in. The patron then walked down a flight of stairs to join the festivities. If he didn't recognize you, good luck.

The Sugar Cane featured a three- or five-piece band, often fronted by a singer, and each musician would occasionally "take a Boston," a solo riff. The patrons were mostly working-class Black men and women out for a good time who liked to dance either "on a dime" or the "bump and mess-around." Champagne and other name-brand liquors were decidedly not available; patrons drank low-grade bootlegged liquor and bathtub concoctions. Wallace Thurman, the noted Harlem Renaissance writer and a club regular, called these patrons "animal beings urged on by liquor and music and physical contact."[119]

Like other Harlem nightspots, the waiters at the Sugar Cane were part of the evening's entertainment. They sang and, according to Ottley, "threaded their incredible way through packed houses, twirling trays aloft, balancing them precariously on one or two fingers, while they danced skillfully between the tables." Looking for recognition, "they executed a dexterous flourish of the tray; an intricate flurry of taps, and deposited a pitcher of raw gin before the customer. 'Yeah, man!'" Another popular nightspot was the Bamboo Inn, on 7th Avenue. It was a speak where, according to a regular, "the place to see 'high Harlem'...well-dressed men escorting expensively garbed women and girls; models from *Vanity Fair*, with brown, yellow, and black skins."

Many legitimate businesses along Lenox Avenue, whether a delicatessen, shoe shop, newsstand, stationery store, soda fountain, cigar store or drugstore, sold cheap (and often home-brewed) alcoholic concoctions. However, a local temperance magazine warned that drinking bathtub gin was like playing Russian roulette: you risked your life. It claimed that a bottle of locally brewed hooch might contain soap, wood alcohol, benzene, kerosene, pyridine, camphor, nicotine, benzyl, formaldehyde, iodine, glycerin or sulfuric acid.

Uptown, other illicit substances were also available. Willie "Suicide" Jones, a former Cotton Club regular, admitted that "performers would smoke [marijuana] outside, because the management wouldn't tolerate it. We used to go to what we called tea pads." He added, "One of the favorite hangouts was right next door in Hoskins', who was the superintendent of 646 and Lenox. He used to serve corn whiskey and peach brandy and reefers."[120] Speakeasies were everywhere.

After the White-only nightclubs closed, African American regulars moved to their favorite after-hours spots. Eddie Barefield, a big-band saxophonist, headed over to a local dive called Mike's. "All the show people from the different shows went there," he recalled. "We just sat around. Sometimes we did some jammin'. The musicians I knew played for musicians. There were always competitions." Ellington preferred Mexico's. Named after its owner's nickname, this speak was, Ellington claimed, "the hottest gin mill on 133rd Street." He added, "You were always seeing cats walking along the street, tubas on shoulders, over to his [Mexico's] cutting contests."[121] The Drool Inn was another notorious dive. Walker, a well-traveled night owl, found "the fun was excruciatingly low-down."

Uptown Parties

In Harlem and other African Americans neighborhoods in the North, speakeasies often were part of house or "rent" parties that took place at "buffet flats." In the days preceding a party, business card announcements were passed out, often through madams, to attract both locals and transient visitors. A sample announcement read:

Hey! Hey!
Come on boys and girls let's shake that
thing
Where?
At
Hot Poppa Sam's
West 134th Street, three flights up
Jelly Roll Smith on the piano
Saturday night…
Hey! Hey![122]

These gatherings, also called "parlor socials," attracted a diverse group of partygoers. In addition to Pullman porters and truck drivers just passing through the city, there were ordinary tradesmen, housemaids, seamstresses, porters, elevator operators and shoeshine boys—as well as writers, artists, musicians, hookers and gangsters.

Patrons were charged fifteen cents to a quarter to get in, and food, drink and everything else was extra. Ottley regularly attended such get-togethers and gives an insider's sense of what took place at one such event. The apartment was "a small bare room with a red glow for light served as the 'ballroom,' where the strenuous business of rug-cuttin' was performed." He added: "The only furniture from which a 'box-beater' extracted close harmonies and 'jump rhythms,' or 'gutbucket,' which is now called boogie-woogie." In the kitchen, chitterlings and pigs were cooking on the stove. Corn whiskey was sold in half-pint portions called "shorties." Wistfully, he noted, "Then there would be goings-on until daybreak, and rent next day for the landlord."[123]

A forgotten ditty captures the spirit of such parties:

There'll be brownskin mammas,
High yellers too,
And if you ain't got nothing to do

Come on up to Mary Lou's.
There'll be plenty of pig feet
And lots of gin;
Jus' ring the bell
An' come on in.[124]

Some of these parties offered "sex circuses" and other illicit attractions.

One could go to a rent party simply to socialize and have a good time. Thurman partied til all hours and had a lot of fun. He danced the now all-but-forgotten "mess around," which he called "a body dance." He found couples "standing transfixed beneath the solitary red glob[e] which provides the light: they bounce on the balls of their feet, which the mid-section of their bodies go round and round."[125] The mixing of dance styles seems to have been common, as Thurman observed "still another couple is doing the 'fish tail' dipping to the floor and slowly shimmying into an upright position then madly whirling a moment before settling into a methodical slow drag one-step."

For Willie the Lion Smith, "The rent party was the place to go to pick up on all the latest jokes, jive, and uptown news. You would see all kinds of people making the party scene." These parties often attracted high-caliber performers like Ellington, Eubie Blake, James P. Johnson and Fats Waller and resulted in fierce competition or "cut sessions." As Smith recalled, "Sometimes we got carving battles going that would last four or five hours.... Hard cash was bet on the outcome and more than once [the listeners would] get ready to fight between them as to who had won."[126] "During these early hours close to dawn the dancers would grab each other and do the monkey hunch or bo-hog," Smith reminisced. "The lights would be dimmed down and the people would call out to the piano player, 'Play it, oh, play it,' or 'Break it down,' or 'Get in the gully and give us the everlovin' stomp.'" And, as Smith wistfully reflected, "Those were happy days."

7

PARTY TIME IN THE OTHER GOTHAM

New York is a city of five boroughs, but all too often for locals and visitors, the city means Manhattan. During Prohibition, New Yorkers in the city and the other four boroughs—Brooklyn, the Bronx, Queens and Staten Island—enjoyed visiting speakeasies and drinking illegal hooch, thus breaking the law. Texas Guinan was very much a wet zone city woman who appears to never have visited speaks in the outer boroughs. Many of the city's beer breweries were founded by German immigrants, and they faced considerable resentment during World War I when nationalists targeted anything German, including an informal boycott of German beers.

In 1920, when Prohibition went into effect, Manhattan's population made up two-fifths (41 percent or 2.3 million) of the city's 5.6 million inhabitants. The other city, the outer boroughs, made up nearly three-fifths of the city's population, with Brooklyn at 2 million and the Bronx at 732,000, while Queens and Staten Island, still largely underdeveloped, had populations of 469,000 and 117,000, respectively. As could be expected, speakeasies flourished in each borough proportional to the population.[127]

BROOKLYN

To get a feel of a Brooklyn '20s speak today visit Monte's at 451 Carroll Street, in the Gowanus neighborhood. It was opened by Angelo and

Filomena Montemarano as Angelo's Tavern in 1906 and the couple lived with their children in an upstairs apartment, growing vegetable in the backyard. During the '20s, it was a speakeasy with a chute in the basement so staff could dump alcohol bottles in case of a police raid.[128]

Brooklyn drinkers long loved to drink. One of its most celebrated breweries was the Edelbrew Brewery at 1 Bushwick Place, in the Williamsburg neighborhood. Edelbrew was founded by a German immigrant, Otto Huber Sr., and after his death in 1889, his sons—Otto, Jr., Joseph, Charles and Max—ran it until the 1920s, when it was sold to Edward Hittleman, who renamed the brewery after himself. Hittleman produced near beer—about 0.5 percent alcohol by volume—until the repeal of Prohibition. In 1934, the brewery's name was changed to Hittleman-Goldenrod Brewery, and it produced once popular brands Goldenrod and Edelbrau (renamed Edelbrew). The brewery closed after Hittleman's death in 1951.[129]

The Bedford Nest at 1286 Bedford Avenue, in the Bedford-Stuyvesant neighborhood, was one of Brooklyn's most infamous speakeasies and regularly raided, included on February 17, 1930. The *Brooklyn Daily Eagle* claimed that "there had been no cessation of drinking in the State and that the number of speakeasies had been holding its own, if not increasing."[130]

Brooklyn drinking was long anchored in two major port areas: on the East River, in the Vinegar Hill neighborhood, and along the Upper New York Bay, in Sunset Park. On the East River, the Brooklyn Navy Yard opened in 1801 and was the scene of a notorious battle in what was known as the Whiskey Wars.[131] In October 1869, the first major temperance war started. It was followed, on November 2, 1870, when U.S. military battalions streamed from the yard and attacked breweries and drinking establishment in Vinegar Hill. U.S. soldiers and sailors—armed with muskets, axes and crowbars—raided some twenty illegal distilleries, leaving them in ruin. Half a century later, a new war against evil alcohol broke out, also targeting Vinegar Hill speaks, and it was no more successful than the earlier one.

As part of its World War I effort, the U.S. government opened the Brooklyn Army Terminal in 1918. Located in the Sunset Park neighborhood, it runs along the Upper New York Bay in the southwest section of Brooklyn. Sunset Park has long been home to immigrants, including Irish, Poles, Norwegians, Italians and Finns, many who found jobs in the shipyards and related businesses. In the '20s, the Bureau of Prohibition used the terminal to store seized alcohol. According to one report, "tens of millions of dollars' worth of beer, whisky, champagne, and more was stored at the base. And much of it, to the chagrin of drinkers everywhere, was dumped—some right over the railroad tracks in the atrium, but most of it straight into New York Harbor."[132]

Al Capone (1929). *Wikimedia Commons.*

In 1927, the *Brooklyn Daily Eagle* called the terminal a "pier of many sorrows" where bootleggers "break the necks off the bottles and they pour the contents into the sea and the mermaids and the fishes enjoy the life of Riley." However, in September 1927, Prohibition agents found that some bootleggers placed metal buckets underneath the pier's wooden planks to capture the lost liquor. According to one scholar, "Inside them was a revolting mixture of liquor, wine, beer, and broken glass, which the bootleggers would periodically collect by rowing a small boat beneath the pier at high tide."[133] Ever clever, the bootleggers redistilled the mixture, rebottled it and sold it to unsuspecting drinkers.

Brooklyn's most famous gangland son was Al Capone (1899–1947), who grew up in the Carroll Gardens neighborhood and was married in St. Mary Star of the Sea Church at 468 Court Street. He apparently hung out at the original—and now gentrified—P.J. Hanley's bar and grill at 449 Court Street. In 1920, he relocated to Chicago, where he gained his notoriety. In 1925, he returned to Brooklyn, ostensibly to find medical help for his son, Sonny, who suffered a mysterious ear infection.

However, while visiting the old neighborhood, Capone supposedly helped an old gangster buddy, Frankie Yale (aka Francesco Ioele or Frankie Uale), whose business was being threatened by another gang, the White Hand (aka White Handers), an Irish gang. In '23, the White Hand gang's leader, Wild Bill Lovett, was murdered by Italian mobsters and his brother-in-law, Richard (Peg Leg) Lonergan, took over. As reported in the *Brooklyn Eagle* on December 26, 1925, Lonergan and two associates were murdered in the Adonis Social Club at 154 20th Street, "a dilapidated 'speakeasy club,'" in what is today part of the South Slope. Capone, along with others in his crew, were supposedly still celebrating Christmas when the killings took place; they were arrested but never charged.[134]

This was not the only shootout in Brooklyn during Prohibition. On February 5, 1926, a man named John Daly was shot at Hicks and Amity

Brooklyn speakeasy where John Daly shooting took place at Hicks and Amity Streets, February 5, 1926. *Det. Gilligan, NYPD Collection, NYC Municipal Archives, NYPD 8051c.*

Streets. Curiously, a man named John Daly was found shot and killed at a speakeasy at Irving Place and Van Brunt Street, in Red Hood.[135] On May 16, 1926, twelve men were shot in a wild gun battle in a speakeasy at 127 West 33rd Street in Brooklyn.

The Bronx

The Bronx is the only New York borough that is not an island. The native Siwanoy band of Lenape first called it Rananchqua, while other Native people called it Keskeskeck; the Bronx River was referred to as the Aquahung. Jonas Bronck, a Scandinavian immigrant, established the first settlement in the area as part of the New Netherland colony in 1639.

Like Brooklyn, the Bronx has a long history of popular local breweries. Many of them were clustered in the Melrose neighborhood, which was, until the five boroughs consolidated in 1898, an unincorporated village in Westchester County. In 1850, the Haffen Brewery—at 152nd Street between Melrose and Courtlandt Avenues—was established. It was founded by Matthias Haffen, a Bavarian immigrant; his son, Louis F. Haffen, was the Bronx's first borough president from 1898 to 1909. Two other breweries were located not far from Haffen's along St. Ann's Avenue between 156th and 161st Streets—Ebling's Brewery and Hupfel's Brewery. Just north in the Morrisania neighborhood, along 3rd Avenue between 168th and 170th Streets,

Homicide of Thomas Reddington, found dead at 474 Brook Avenue, Bronx (a speakeasy), April 9, 1927. *George B. Nolan, NYPD Collection, NYC Municipal Archives, NYPD 8926a.*

four additional breweries operated: Mayer's Brewery, North Side Brewery, Eichler's Brewery and Zeltner's Brewery.[136]

Prohibition took its toll on the Bronx, especially on the breweries. Hupfel's went into the mushroom farming business but eventually closed as did the North Side Brewery and Zeltner's. Ebling's, Eichler's and Mayer's stayed alive offering legal .5 percent ABV. As one scholar noted, "It was an end of an era and a way of life for so many Bronxites who's [*sic*] livelihoods depended on the beer industry."[137]

Like Manhattan and Brooklyn, Prohibition led to the growth of underworld gangs in the Bronx. Immigrant Irish, Jewish, Polish and Italians dominated the illegal distribution of smuggled liquor trade in the Bronx. And none was more pivotal to crime in the Bronx than Dutch Schultz (1902–1935). Born Arthur Flegenheimer to German Jewish immigrant parents, he grew up in the slums of the Bronx. He got his start in the crime racket working as a bouncer and bartender at the Hub Social Club, a speak on Brook Avenue owned by Joey Noe, a smalltime gangster. The two clicked and formed their own gang. In the 1920s, the pair acquired their own trucks for distribution and ran bootlegging operations to Manhattan saloons. Schultz became known as "The Beer Baron of the Bronx."

The Noe-Schultz gang challenged the Rock brothers, John and Joe, a rival Irish gang, for control of the bootlegging operations. Schultz had Joe Rock kidnapped and, while in captivity, hung him from a meat-hook by his thumbs; worse still, according to one report, Schultz personally rubbed gonorrhea pus into the hostage's eyes, permanently blinding him. The Rock family paid $35,000 for his release. Schultz expanded his operations into

Manhattan, coming into conflict with Jack "Legs" Diamond. The conflict escalated. Diamond had Schultz's partner Noey killed; in retaliation, Schultz apparently had Arnold Rothstein murdered. The turf war ended when Schultz's gunman, Abe Weinberg, assassinated Diamond.[138]

According to various reports, Dutch Schultz's illegal operations were very successful. By 1928, his bootlegging operations were grossing $2 million a year worth of alcohol (nearly $30 million in 2020 dollars). One report claims that Schultz "brought in $54,126 of profit per month, or $780,000 in contemporary money." Ever opportunistic, seeing the end of Prohibition coming, Schultz shifted his operations to the gambling racket and operated a slew of slot machines and lotteries until 1933, when the feds indicted him for income tax evasion. He was tried and found not guilty.[139] In 1935, he was assassinated in a Newark, New Jersey club.

Queens

Queens is on Long Island, one borough farther east from Brooklyn. The first European settlements in Queens were land grants awarded by the Dutch and located in the Dutch Kills area of Long Island City. While long underdeveloped, the 1920s saw the Queens population more than double, from 469,042 to 1,079,129 in 1930.[140] And like other boroughs, many Queens residents liked to drink.

Before Prohibition, the Queens neighborhoods of Ridgewood and Glendale were home to many breweries and local restaurants, taverns and inns welcoming drinkers. Among the popular watering holes were Liebmann Breweries Inc.; some accounts place Liebmann Breweries in Brooklyn. It operated between 1920 and 1964, gaining popularity with its Rheingold Beer. It organized an annual Miss Rheingold beauty contest that was featured in ads and billboards, including the city's subway. However, during Prohibition, it produced near beer. Diogenes Brewery, located at the corner of Wyckoff Avenue and present-day Decatur Street, became the Malt-Diataste Company, shifting from beer to malt syrup. The Frank Brewery, located at Cypress Avenue and Hancock Street, and the City Brewing Company closed during Prohibition; City Brewing reopened after Prohibition's repeal.

Like other city breweries, a number of Queens breweries operated their own restaurants. For example, Liebmann's Sons Brewing Company

Broad Channel. *New York Public Library, the Miriam and Ira D. Wallach Division of Art, Prints and Photographs: Picture Collection, Shelf locator: PC POC NEW YC-Que.*

operated a saloon at 770 Onderdonk Avenue that closed during Prohibition; it reopened following repeal as Two Kioodles bar (*Kioodles* is German for "dogs"). Another popular watering hole was the Brockmann Brothers' hotel and saloon, located at Myrtle Avenue and 69th Place in the Glendale neighborhood; it stopped offering alcohol beverages during Prohibition and was became the Brockman Brothers Restaurant.[141]

During Prohibition, Broad Channel was one of the centers of alcohol smuggling. Located in southern Queens on Rulers Bar Hassock, it was the only inhabited island in Jamaica Bay. It offered discreet landing places for liquor smugglers due the long docks full of fishing and yacht clubs, many with trapdoors to receive the hooch. It acquired the nickname "Little Cuba" because of all the rum that passed through it. In one report, a boat was seized at Beach 97 Street with four hundred cases of scotch whiskey. Another popular tale claims that when a revenuer came searching for illegal liquor, one speakeasy would be designated to take the fall. There was no vehicular connection between Broad Channel and the rest of the city until 1925, when the Cross Bay Boulevard was built. Nevertheless, during the '20s, local establishments got very popular, including Hermit's Café, which welcomed Mae West and Jimmy Durante. In the 1930s, Broad Channel became a year-round community following the construction and widening of Cross Bay Boulevard.[142]

Before the imposition of Prohibition, Queens parks welcomed beer drinkers. Schmidt's Woods, a twenty-six-acre park then at Myrtle Avenue and 83rd Street in the Glendale neighborhood, had swings for children, baseball fields and a soccer field. It also had picnic tables that drew families for festive weekend get-togethers. One of the popular beers available was the Welz and Zerwick lager; an eighth of a barrel cost one dollar, and free salty pretzels were often provided to keep drinkers coming back for more beer. The park was closed in 1925 and the land redeveloped for housing.[143]

In 1931, Governor Franklin Roosevelt pushed the New York State legislature to form a joint legislative committee to investigate corruption in the city's magistrate's courts and police department. The Hofstadter Committee was led by Judge Samuel Seabury and revealed an extensive illegal liquor syndicate operating in Jamaica, Queens. It operated a distillery out of a former piano factory building and included rogue police officials on the take. This and other revelations forced the resignation of Mayor Walker.

8
SEX AND OTHER PLEASURES

Sexual Transgression

Mabel Hamilton was an African American chorus girl who regularly performed in Coney Island, around Greenwich Village and at Harlem's Lafayette Theatre. As a Roaring Twenties new woman, she attended some of the more refined "sex circuses," including one hosted by A'Lelia Walker, the millionaire daughter of the legendary businesswoman Madame C.J. Walker.

One evening, Hamilton rang the doorbell at 108–10 West 136th Street, a fashionable brownstone in the heart of Harlem's Sugar Hill. It was Walker's home, and after a patient ten minutes, the owner opened the door, wearing only a maroon robe and slippers. Walker warmly greeted the visitor. Following Walker into her uptown mansion, Hamilton entered a well-appointed parlor where a dozen or more naked men and women, Black and White, were lounging provocatively on scattered throw pillows. As one commentator later reported, "Soft music filled the room, gentle lights emanated from the floor, and the men and women lay in each other's arms." Hamilton was not surprised by the fact that "men were lying on top of other men, and women were lying on top of other women."[144] Hamilton, a truly new woman, had no problem joining the festivities.

Sex circuses were also held in buffet flats, uptown apartments rented out for special functions. Though their name suggests genteel-enough origins, buffet flats had, by the '20s, acquired distinctly unzipped connotations. Many were

A'Lelia Walker, American businesswoman and patron of the arts. *Carl Van Vechten/Yale Collection of American Literature, Beinecke Rare Book and Manuscript Library*

grand spectacles hosted by well-known personalities like the pianist David Fountaine and Caska Bonds, a close friend of Madame Walker. Men and women, White "slummers" and Black celebrities, straight and gay patronized these notorious get-togethers—even Cole Porter and Cary Grant made an occasional appearance. However, most were common rent parties organized to raise money to pay the landlord. "Some were raucous establishments where illegal activities such as drinking, gambling, and prostitution were available," Eric Garber found. "Others offered a variety of sexual pleasures cafeteria-style."[145]

Rent parties charged a modest admission fee, and visitors were often treated to the latest pick-up bands playing the hottest jazz. Music was accompanied by suggestive dancing, free-flowing booze and other drugs sold at a steep price. They were a tradition brought from the South with the Great Migration and took place in all the major northern cities. They were private get-togethers; they were sometimes mixed in terms of race and class as well as gender and sexual orientation; and they were sometimes limited to gay men, sometimes to gay women. Most often, they offered privacy and safety from police harassment, thus were one of the few places that heterosexual and homosexual adventurers could gather and have fun, social and sexual. Hamilton met Lillian Foster at a city bus stop and struck up a conversation. She gave Foster a card for a rent party she was throwing, and the two became lovers and partners for over forty years.[146]

In Harlem and other African American neighborhoods, buffet parties were a regular part of the late-night entertainment scene. Blues singer Bessie Smith's niece Ruby Walker recalled that buffet flats serviced "nothing but faggots and bulldykers, a real open house. Everything went on in that house—tongue baths, you name it. They called them buffet flats because buffet meant everything, everything that was in the life."[147]

Polly Adler, a legendary New York madam, regularly attended such gatherings. In her memoir, *A House Is Not a Home*, Adler recalls visiting a party run by Sewing Machine Bertha at which upper-class White visitors out for a night of slumming "would be shown lewd pictures as a preview to the performance of the same tableaux by live actors, white and colored." She reported, "Money also supplied reefers and cocaine and morphine so that the 'upper clawsses' could have themselves a real low-down time."[148] Another famous uptown event that catered to mostly Black patrons, gay and straight of both sexes, was held at the Daisy Chain, aka the 101 Ranch, Hazel Valentine's place on 148th Street. It featured entertainers such as the multitalented Sewing Machine Bertha and an enormous trans person named Clarenz. Such was the Daisy Chain's celebrity that both Fats Waller and Count Basie composed tunes commemorating it.

Sex performance parties took place as part of the commercial sex engagements at, for example, the Adam's Theatrical Boarding House on West 128th Street and a tenement call house on West 75th Street run by a woman named Faye. Two unique features of these circuses most acutely expressed America's emerging transgressive sexual culture. First, the heterosexual male customer was openly fascinated watching the female performers' homoerotic engagement; second, there was an unstated requirement that female performers appear to enjoy the sex they engaged in. Women were becoming increasingly commercialized, and the boundaries of acceptable sex were being redrawn.

Speakeasy Sex

Mae West caught the spirit of Prohibition-era sexuality visiting one of Chicago's most notorious speakeasies, the Elite No. 1 Café. Watching Black couples dance the shimmy, she noticed that they "stood in one spot, with hardly any movement of the feet and just shook their shoulders, torsos, breasts and pelvises. We thought it was funny and were terribly amused by it." Being smarter, more honest than many of the other White slummers visiting the club that night, she noted with remarkable pathos, "But there was a naked, aching sensual agony about it too."[149]

"Diamond L'il rides home from Hollywood…World Telegram photo. Mae West, riding in a carriage, on her return from Hollywood." *Wikimedia Commons.*

One of the unintended consequences of Prohibition was the role of speakeasies in the democratization of illicit sex. While slumming had long been an indulgence, if not liberty, of many well-to-do men (and some women), the intimate theaters created by Prohibition brought together elements of normally disparate social groups through a special form of bonding, breaking the law and enjoying it. In the more radical (and often upscale) speaks, men and women, gay and straight, Black and White came together through this shared conspiracy. Other, more local venues catered to mostly poorer, working-class and distinct ethnic or racial minority groups. At all rungs of social transgression, as George Chauncey reminds us, "Prohibition resulted ...in the expansion of the sexual underworld."[150]

During Prohibition, speakeasies provided illegal alcohol and a social opportunity to meet a sex worker. The neighborhood watering hole often drew prostitutes who congregated like other customers and also solicited business. This was the most popular form of speakeasy prostitution and operated throughout the city, often with the complicity of the local beat cop, who received his usual kickback. However, the most notorious sexual venues were speaks that resembled traditional brothels. They often had a back room where commercial sex took place and the prostitutes functioned as "residents" or "sitters."

In many working-class neighborhoods, pre–World War I saloons hung on into the '20s, and prostitutes worked as hostesses, providing either a hurried service in a private booth, an upstairs or back room or left the venue to conduct the sexual encounter at a building cellar or nearby apartment. Sometimes sexual services also took place in clubs where the owner got a kickback from the sex worker. These speaks were referred to as "clip joints" and, as one scholar found, were considered "a step above a whorehouse." Many were described as "sordid" places "haunted by bargirls pushing foul drink in exchange for the promise of spurious sex to come." The entertainer Jimmy Durante put it best: they were spots for "out-of-town buyers and cheating husbands seeking to blow-off steam."[151]

Jimmy Durante. *Wikimedia Commons.*

Chauncey makes the '20s a more complex era by noting that "the social dichotomies of heterosexuality and homosexuality were not yet hegemonic." The social categories that defined male and female sexual identify were not as yet as formal, fixed or exclusionary as they would become in the post World War II era. Male and female sexual categories were in some important ways less restrictive than they are today. As Chauncey reminds us,

> *Many men alternated between male and female sexual partners without believing that interest in one precluded interest in the other, or that their occasional recourse to male sexual partners, in particular, indicated an abnormal, "homosexual," or even "bisexual" disposition, for they neither understood nor organized their sexual practices along a hetero-homosexual axis.*[152]

At the better, upscale venues, sex approximated more respectable heterosexual relations. "Elite white dance hostesses and black women within the upper tier of nightclubs often spent the night with the clients and engaged in traditional intercourse, performing their sexual exchanges in ways that mimicked or emulated noncommercial sexual relations," Kevin Mumford found. "These elite hostesses were something like a middle-class man's mistress; they concealed or denied that commercial aspects and dramatized the affective or romantic dimensions of the exchange."[153] Like alcohol, sex flowed during Prohibition.

Venues of Temptation

During the first decades of the twentieth century, sex became a more explicit commodity, saturating New York society and private life. By the time Prohibition was imposed, venues of erotic temptation had increased significantly. Such venues ranged from sex circuses, movie houses, burlesque theaters, brothels, dance halls, traveling "girl shows" and retail shops offering all manner of "obscene" materials. During Prohibition, illegal alcohol only added to the overall excitement, encouraging flirtation, fantasy and sexual encounters.

By the 1920s, movie theaters were on their way to becoming the dominant cultural medium of the first half of the twentieth century, only to be eclipsed after World War II by television. The growing popularity of movies was combined with more disposable income in many more people's pockets. The led to movie theaters ranging from expensive palaces to more modest neighborhood houses and skid-row dives. In 1922, the forces of moral rectitude, led by the Catholic Church, forced the movie industry to establish the Hays Office to regulate the content of movies. Under the code, movie producers adopted a sophisticated, opportunistic strategy of voicing support for restraint while continuing to produce racy films that violated the code in all but name. Owners undertook a vigorous effort to clean up these previously notorious social spaces, including cutting back on (censoring) the showing of more erotic movies.

Live performances of provocative erotic display by women were the most explicit public expressions of 1920s social transgression. They found their most popular representation in New York speakeasies, like those fronted by Texas Guinan's Graduates and chorus girl shows in Broadway follies. However, burlesque, and especially the legendary female star, was the supreme embodiment of this new sexuality. Burlesque was introduced in America in 1868 and was popular as a live performance art until 1942, mapping out the evolution of the modern female sex star.

Burlesque's original appeal was derived from a very compelling presentation of female identity, one that uniquely combined what Robert Allen calls "sexual allure and inversive feminine insubordination." He appreciated the full power of these two characteristics: "Either half alone could be controlled and made to please without seriously undermining the position of the male spectator. Fused together in a single performer, however, this combination was much more threatening."[154]

In response, and apparently as the result of an intentional "accident," the striptease emerged during the late 1910s and, by the '20s, had become the principal form of presentation. It appears to have made its first public display at the St. Louis exposition of 1896, when Omeena performed what was called the "take off."[155] As legend has it, the first "strip" took place at the Minsky Brothers' New York burlesque theater. Allen recounts this memorable moment:

> *In 1917 they constructed a runway into the auditorium so that patrons could examine cooch dancers more closely....May Dix did her dance act in a short black dress with detachable white collar and cuffs. At the end of her song one hot summer night, she removed her collar as she walked offstage, trying to forestall the next laundry bill. Someone in the audience demanded an encore, at the end of which she removed her cuffs as well. "Between the heat and the applause* [reported Morton Minsky], *May lost her head, went back for a short chorus, and unbuttoned her bodice as she left the stage again.*

It was, as Allen concludes, "burlesque's last-ditch and ultimately unsuccessful strategy to stay alive."[156]

Faith Bacon, portrait by John de Mirjian (before 1929). *Wikimedia Commons.*

With the adoption of the striptease, the female star was transformed. Her sexual allure became the predominant, if not sole, source of her appeal, as represented by the fan dancer, notably Sally Rand and Faith Bacon. As the male audience's attention became more and more fixed on her ever more nude body, the female performer lost her equally compelling attraction, her spirit of insubordination. With the striptease, the female object of desire was silenced, her transgressive appeal reduced to an image parading before the paying male customer. By 1923, as *Variety* reported, burlesque had become "ninety-nine percent strip with the other just to pad out the show."

The dance halls of the early twentieth century were popular social spaces for flirtation and sexual engagement. "The gaily decorated hall, riveting beat of the orchestra, and dance partners created," in the words of one historian, "a magical world of pleasure and romance." In the '20s, dances and balls were phenomenally popular in New York and other cities. They were held on a nightly basis in a wide variety of spaces and catered to all social classes, races and ethnic groups. Venues ranged from dingy saloon backrooms and walkups to religious, fraternal, trade union and neighborhood halls and well-lit commercial pavilions and ballrooms. While few openly sold alcohol, many dance halls winked approvingly at the flask carried by the hipster.

According to legend, taxi-dance halls emerged in San Francisco in the late-nineteenth century and, by the 1920s, were a nationwide phenomenon. These heterosexual gathering places permitted what was then referred to as "erotic" or "sensual" dancing, encouraging the female dancers to engage in suggestive body-rubbing, touching, the use of provocative language and even masturbation to bring the male customer to orgasm. And all was done without intercourse. As one female performer warned an investigator, she could "starch your underwear."

Taxi-dance halls got their name from a hack or taxi driver running the meter. They took place in a formal dance hall setting with a live band or orchestra performing. The male patron was expected to purchase tickets that he turned over to the female dancer when the song finished; she in turn redeemed them for cash, less attendant costs. "Because the dances were so short, and the band hardly paused between them," reports Elizabeth Clement, "a series of lights above the orchestra indicated to the dancers how many dances had gone by."[157] It took a man between five to eight dances to ejaculate.

What makes these establishments even more remarkable was how, during the '20s, they had become identified with interracial mixing, especially between Asian and other immigrant men and White women. In cities with significant Chinese, Filipino, Japanese, Italian or Spanish communities, and especially those with an overwhelming number of men like San Francisco, Chicago and New York, taxi-dance halls provided one of the only social venues for single men to associate with women and to engage in a sexual encounter, however limited it might be. In New York, clubs like the Rainbow Garden (on East 125th Street), Sunbeam Dance Palace, Happyland Dance Academy, Lincoln Square Dancing and Goldman's Dance Hall enabled men to obtain sexual release at a relatively low price. While there were extensive reports of these men being overcharged, insulted and taken advantage of, it was only here that they could socially (let alone sexually) engage with a woman for as little as two to three dollars as compared to the twenty dollars or more it cost to spend time with a prostitute.

The traveling girl show was yet another venue of female sexual display but one that rarely visited the Big Apple. It emerged out of the Chicago Exposition of 1893, and by 1920, there were an estimated two hundred operating nationally. The "girls" who worked in these shows performed a variety of provocative sex acts. As Allen observes:

> *Girl shows are distinguished by how "strong" the dancers are allowed to perform—in other words, by the extent of sexual abandon of the dancing routines and the degree of genital display. In the large and more sedate carnivals (those that play state fair dates, for example), the performance might end with a strip down to the G-string or its removal for a moment just before the dancer leaves the stage. In the smaller shows, however, where "stronger" acts are the norm, the performance might end with a gynecological anatomy lesson.*[158]

The show's female posture artist acted out a "Living Picture," in which she held a revealing pose (often with minimal clothing) for audience inspection and performed some suggestive dances, including the "Butterfly" and the "Serpentine." Utilizing the artful technique called the "girls and grift" con, the carney operator further tapped male desire with the suggestive fantasy of the "cooch" dance. After seeing the more public show, and for an additional fee, marks would be invited into back rooms where the girls put on a special show.[159]

During Prohibition and for much of the twentieth century, Gotham was the capital of the pornography industry, particularly print pornography. "[T]he 1920s and 1930s," reports Jay A. Gertzman, "produced an unprecedented amount of erotica in America." Illegally printed sexual materials fell broadly into two categories, art (i.e., obscenity) and erotica (i.e., pornography). The difference between them, according to Gertzman, "was mostly a matter of marketing convenience." People who were interested in such material had a wide variety to choose from.

The "sex pulps" were the erotic equivalent of popular pulp magazines that included gossip, pinup art and nudist publications like *Broadway Brevities*, *Police Gazette*, *Artists and Models* and *Paris Nights*. They "featured brightly colored jackets, plain cloth bindings, inexpensive paper, and were small enough to be held in one hand as part of a cigar or drugstore shopper's purchase." More to the point, Gertzman points out: They were "aggressive rather than discreetly titillating, parvenu rather than genteel in sensibility, garish rather than sophisticated in their packaging, and issued in large print runs rather than limited editions." No wonder they were popular among both men and women.

Eight-page comic books dubbed "bibles" and "readers"—like the popular "Tijuana bibles"—were cheaply produced, often side-stapled, erotic works. They were often sexual parodies of popular newspaper comic-strip characters or famous theater or movie stars, including Orphan Annie, "Mae Breast"

Cover of a circa 1936 Tijuana bible: *The Adventures of a Fuller Brush Man* (non-offensive). *Wikimedia Commons.*

and "Douglas Farybanks," and they were often sold under the counter at speakeasies. Finally, sexology or "erotology" represented the more academic or scholarly segment of erotica and focused on the techniques of sexual stimulation. It included sex encyclopedias, medical treatises on the benefits of flagellation and other sexual practices, "scientific" studies of sexual variations both legendary and anthropological and similar topics.[160]

The brothel was still another venue for erotic engagement. Polly Adler began her career as a New York madam during the Roaring Twenties. By the 1930s and '40s, she was renowned for running some of the city's most fashionable, upscale—and completely illegal—brothels. Adler, a small woman standing only four feet, eleven inches was a spitfire who found her way into the prostitution racket by chance. As she recounts in her entertaining autobiography, *A House Is Not a Home*, good fortune enabled her to move in with a young woman living in an apartment on Riverside Drive on the Upper West Side and meet actresses, showgirls and gangsters. In 1922, a bootlegger hired her as a procurer of women, and she started to freelance:

> *Soon I was meeting a lot of money men and when I saw the way they flung dough around I thought to myself: Why shouldn't some of it be flung my way?...So I gave my address to the one who I thought would be discreet, and it wasn't long before three girls were coming in several nights a week to entertain acquaintances I had made along the Great White Way.*[161]

She got busted in a police raid running her first "disorderly house." After a failed effort running a lingerie shop, she returned to her "calling."

Prostitutes operating out of a speakeasy tended to engage in a limited range of sexual practices. Most often these women provided their male customers fellatio, with only a small fraction willing to engage in coitus. Kevin Mumford's assessment of sex in Chicago speaks can be applied to New York: "Speakeasy sex was performed in corners of dark hallways, beneath a staircase, behind a trash bin in an alley....It was aggressive, quick, groping, highly impersonal, stripped of any pretense of Victorian romance." He adds: "African-American female prostitutes performed the kind of sexual services that were deemed most degenerate, most immoral, the least 'domestic,' and, for some, the most desirable." Looking specifically at the nature of the emotional costs of the sex conducted by Black prostitutes in a Harlem or Chicago tenement speakeasy, Mumford warns that they "represented the ultimate example of modern anomie, of bodily interpenetration and complete emotional estrangement."

9
PANSY CITY

PANSY BALLS

New York nightlife during the Roaring Twenties drew many unlikely people together, enriching cultural life—often enhanced with the pleasures of illegal alcohol. Two people who did cross paths during the '20s were Texas Guinan and Carl Van Vechten. In some important ways, their lives were not that dissimilar. They shared complementary expressions of a common impulse, the lure of the illicit. Neither was a born-and-bred New Yorker but came from faraway, small-town America seeking—and achieving—celebrity stardom in Gotham. What Tex signified in term of nightlife, Van Vechten represented in terms of literary life.

Forgotten today, Van Vechten was a popular figure in the Gotham literary and nightlife scenes of the 1920s and '30s. He was a former arts critic at the *New York Times* and *New York Press* as well as the author of a half-dozen novels, including the '20s classic *Nigger Heaven*, a best-seller with fourteen print runs and one of the most controversial novels of the era. But most importantly, he was a well-to-do man-about-town, a well-known married man who enjoyed bisexual dalliances and indulged in interracial homoerotic pleasures. He was White Gotham's cultural ambassador to the Harlem Renaissance, helping many leading African American writers get published.

On a given night, he might have been a celebrity judge at a drag ball with a fellow judge like prizefighter Jack Johnson or the entertainer Ethel

Right: A Carl Van Vechten, 1932. *Library of Congress Prints and Photographs Division, Reproduction Number LOT 12735, no. 1122 [P&P].*

Below: Drag ball in Webster Hall (1920s). *Wikimedia Commons.*

Waters. It was an event that Texas would never have attended. The evening's entertainment opened with an orchestra playing and attendees dancing. Participants dressed in grand style, everything from Marie Antoinette costumes, feathered gowns and plumed headdresses to men's and women's formalwear.

After the festive warm-up, the event organizers would clear the floor and invite the contestants to assemble and parade at center-stage in front of a committee of judges. The judges then stepped forward, carefully considering the contestants and made a first cut, selecting the finalists. The finalists joined in what was known as the "parade of fairies," strolling before the judges and the evening's clamorous attendees. According to one historian, those in attendance, judges and attendees together, would "determine the most unique, glamorous, and graceful of the 'fairies' to cross the stage."[162] The winner was chosen by attendee applause and shouts of approval and was often awarded a cash prize, sometimes as much as $200 (about $2,700 in 2020 dollars).

Speakeasy drag shows grew out of masquerade balls long held in New York, Chicago, Baltimore and New Orleans. They, in turn, harkened back to the *bals masqués* fashionable during the high Victorian era. Early twentieth-century balls were notorious, in the words of one astute observer, for the "promiscuous intermingling" they encouraged, thus serving as "liminal cultural spaces in which people could transgress."[163]

Drag Shows

George Chauncey found that during Prohibition, drag balls became "the largest and most signific collective events in gay society." By the mid-'20s, a half-dozen enormous balls were being staged annually in some of New York's most prestigious civic venues, including Madison Square Garden, the Astor Hotel and the Manhattan Casino in midtown and Harlem's Savoy Ballroom. As Chauncey reports, "The Vanderbilts, the Astors, and other pillars of respectability were often there, along with Broadway celebrities popular in the gay world, such as Beatrice Lillie, Clifton Webb, Jay Brennan, and Tallulah Bankhead."[164] However, the most spectacular costume balls were held at the cavernous Rockland Palace at 280 West 155th Street and 8th Avenue.

Explicitly Afro-American gay balls had their origin in the annual galas held, beginning in 1869, at New York's Hamilton Lodge No. 710 of the Grand United Order of the Odd Fellows. These events were so popular that at their peak, at the Hamilton Lodge alone, attendance rose from 800 in 1925 to 1,500 in 1926 and to an estimated 8,000 in 1932; by 1937, as the Depression hit rock-bottom, attendance had dropped to a "mere" 4,000. "Great fun was to be had, after all....Solidarity of a kind was possible, and strength in numbers did mean something at least for the night," acknowledges Chauncey. "Even class barriers were momentarily lifted."

Most exciting for those in attendance, the drag balls drew an immensely varied crowd. A singer of the day described one as "packed with people from bootblacks to New York's rarest bluebloods." "Although whites attended the [Hamilton] ball as both dancers and spectators, most of the guests were black." Even the sexual orientation of the guests was not uniform: "Lesbian 'male impersonators' and straight masqueraders attended as well as gay men, but the latter constituted the vast majority of dancers and the focal point of attention."

In the late 1920s, as Prohibition was in its final phase, Harlem's cavernous Rockland Palace hosted the most spectacular costume balls. In 1928, *Variety* reported that at 12:30 am, a New York policeman "visited and found approximately 5,000 people, colored and white, men attired in women's clothing, and vice versa." The officer went on to explain that the affair "was a Fag (fairy) Masquerade Ball." *Variety* added, for the benefit of the uninitiated, "This is an annual affair where the white and colored fairies assemble together with their friends, this being attended also by certain respectable elements who go there to see the sights."[165]

An observant *New York Herald Tribune* reporter attended a drag ball at the Rockland Palace in 1932. "Blonds equipped themselves with dark hair," he reported. More shocking, "[C]aucasians came distinguished as Orientals. Mongoloid individuals blackened their faces and appeared as Ethiopians. Negroes powdered their skins and dressed as Scandinavian villagers. College boys masqueraded as hoboes. Waitresses and soda clerks wore full evening dresses." Attuned to the changing sexual mores of the period, he acknowledged the even more radical sexuality at the heart of the evening's festivities. "Men danced with women in men's clothes. Women danced with men in women's clothes," he found. "And strange androgynous couples careened about the floor oblivious to the workings of society and nature."[166]

That same year, a reporter for the Black-owned *Pittsburgh Courier* reported on the goings-on at the Rockland Palace. "Men danced with men, women

Left: Langston Hughes, Carl Van Vechten *portrait, 1936. Library of Congress Control Number 2004664043.*

Right: Gladys Bentley. *Wikimedia Commons.*

danced with women. An occasional heated love affair was observed in the corners and crevices of Rockland Palace." Intrigued, it went on, "In the dark corners of the balcony of the ballroom several couples were seen making love in a most amorous way." Captivated, the reporter offered some spicy details: "Love flared hot and quick…[and] men openly kissed and caressed one another, and women likewise."[167]

Langston Hughes, the celebrated Harlem Renaissance poet, attended Rockland Palace masquerade galas, at least once accompanied by A'Lelia Walker, the queen of Harlem nightlife. "It is," he reports, "the ball where men dress up as women and women dress up as men." He dubbed these promiscuous get-togethers, "spectacles in color," where "it was fashionable for the intelligentsia and social leaders of both Harlem and the downtown area to occupy boxes at this ball and look down from above at the queerly assorted throng on the dancing floor." Looking out from Madame Walker's special box, he observed "males in flowing gowns and feathered headdresses and females in tuxedoes and box-back suits."[168]

In 1928, Van Vechten visited the Lulu Belle Club, a notorious drag club located at 341 Lenox Avenue, near 127th Street, at least three times. He also developed an apparently deeply felt and long-term friendship with the club's star attraction, Gladys Bentley. Known affectionately as "La Bentley," she was a large-bodied—some say 250 pounds, 300 pounds, 400 pounds, who knows—African American lesbian performer who famously dressed in a white tuxedo and top hat. On January 29, 1928, the Lulu Belle Club was raided, sixty-three people were busted, and the club was closed. According to the *New York Times*, "most of those arrested were white persons who said they had been slumming." Later that year, the club reopened, and Van Vechten attended the festivities. That evening, he was accompanied by Louis Cole, whom historian James Wilson identifies as a "black entertainer who sometimes appeared in drag." The partygoers stayed until three o'clock in the morning.[169]

At "Legs" Diamond's Club Abbey, located in the Hotel Harding at 203 West 54th Street, the popular drag entertainer Malin performed with a chorus line of "pansy" showgirls. The Pansy Club was located a couple blocks south, at 48th Street and Broadway, next door to Niles Granlund's famous Hollywood Restaurant, in the heart of the wet zone. Karyl Norman, popularly known as the Creole Fashion Plate, was the club's mistress of ceremonies. Born George Peduzzi in Baltimore, Maryland, Norman performed widely on the circuits in the United States, Europe and Australia. Remarkably, he performed both in and out of drag. Moving to Los Angeles, he appeared in the 1933 movie *Arizona to Broadway* and died the same year in a car crash.

The Abbey and the Pansy Club were but two of a network of ribald late-night gay clubs that flourished during Prohibition in the wet zone, Greenwich Village, Harlem and other parts of the city. Many featured campy cabaret shows, men in drag decked out as the most glamorous female stars of the day, including Sophie Tucker and Mae West. All facilitated a radical sexuality. Stanley Walker warned, "The police, with their traditional hatred of the intermediate sex, kept their nightsticks poised."[170]

In Harlem, among the haunts that welcomed gay patrons and slummers were the Garden of Joy and the Yeahman, sometimes spelled Yeah Man, at 135th Street and 7th Avenue. The Garden of Joy was an open-air Harlem dance hall with canvas sides walls located on top of a rock shelf on 7th Avenue between 138th and 139th Streets. Founded by blues singer Mamie Smith, it was a popular afternoon spot often called "the Rock."

In 1928, Mr. Winston was hostess at the Book Store, a cellar club on 134th Street, and appeared to popular acclaim as Gloria Swanson.

According to Bruce Nugent, a Renaissance writer and painter, Winston's "public life was lived in evening gowns, his private life in boa-trimmed negligees." The scene at the Book Store speaks to his appeal. As Nugent recalls, "He had the free load camaraderie that distinguished the famous Texas Guinan." Nugent acknowledged that "gangsters and hoodlums, pimps and gamblers, whores and entertainers showered him with feminine geegaws, spoke of him as 'her,' and quite enthusiastically relegated him to the female's functions of supplying good times and entertainment." Never losing his sense of humor, Nugent acknowledged, "He [Mr. Winston] could also cook." Herman Warner, a Jamaican doctor who practiced in Harlem, fondly recalled the Book Store. "Gloria Swanson used to sing a song called 'Hot Nuts.' The song was 'Hot nuts, get 'em from the peanut man.' As soon as you would enter, he would make you sing the song: 'Hot nuts, tell it to the peanut man. You see that man walking here in green? He has good nuts be won't keep 'em clean.'"[171]

The Clam House featured Gladys Bentley, known affectionately as La Bentley. Her famous song, "My Subway Man," featured, in the words of one commentator, "some of the naughtier lyrics of the decade." The speak was run by Harry Hansberry and was a long, narrow room on 133rd Street's Jungle Alley.[172] *Vanity Fair* described it as "a popular house for revelers but not for the innocent young." Bentley also sang popular songs like "My Alice Blue Gown" and "Sweet Georgia Brown" and encouraged the club's patrons to join in the festivities. It was so popular that downtown celebrities like Beatrice Lillie and Tallulah Bankhead regularly visited.

The onset of the Great Depression, FDR's election and the repeal of Prohibition in 1933 ended the revelry of the Roaring Twenties and the social revolution it fostered. As unemployment increased, so too did homelessness and hunger. With no money in the male wage earner's pocket, domestic violence, evictions and family abandonments skyrocketed. Masculinity faced a historically unprecedented crisis. One consequence of the new, darker times was a campaign against homosexuals, especially the more "out" or publicly visible gay men. Following LaGuardia's election in 1933, the city passed an ordinance banning drag queens from 14th to 72nd Streets, thus introducing a new era in Gotham's illicit sex scene.

White Man in Harlem

One warm night in June 1925, an invited group of celebrated New Yorkers gathered for a regular salon hosted by Van Vechten and Fania Marinoff at their fashionable apartment at 150 West 55th Street. This night was special because it featured George Gershwin playing show tunes at the piano, followed by Paul Robeson singing Black spirituals and ended with James Weldon Johnson reciting "Go Down, Death," a funeral dirge. It reads, in part:

And Death heard the summons,
And he leaped on his fastest horse,
Pale as a sheet in the moonlight.
Up the golden street Death galloped,
And the hooves of his horses struck fire from the gold,
But they didn't make no sound.
Up Death rode to the Great White Throne,
And waited for God's command.

At the soirées Van Vechten hosted, his regular bootlegger, Jack Harper, supplied the illegal alcohol.[173] Van Vechten played an unprecedented role in the city's cultural life. He was an indefatigable schmoozer who knew everyone who was in the know, from Salvador Dalí to W.E.B. DuBois, from Theodore Dreiser to Helena Rubinstein. He was a popular figure in the city's literary scene, a critic at the *New York Times* and *New York Press*, a regular contributor to *Vanity Fair* and a popular novelist; later in life, he became an accomplished photographer. Bequeathed a sizable inheritance by his brother and tiring of the grind of a newspaper critic, Van Vechten became a freelance writer and a '20s man-about-town.

Van Vechten helped innumerable Black artists achieve recognition they might have never received without his intervention. Among them were the literary figures Johnson, Hughes, Hurston, Wallace Thurman, Walter White, Countee Cullen, Nella Larsen and Rudolf Fisher; the artist Aaron Douglas; and the legendary blues singers Bessie Smith and Ethel Waters.[174] Van Vechten's network boasted friendships with Scott and Zelda Fitzgerald, who served as models for his novel *Parties*.[175] He also had a long-term professional and personal association with the important publisher Alfred Knopf and his wife, Blanche. He introduced Margaret Anderson, founder of quintessential '20s journal *The Little Review*, to his uptown friends; she published Jean Toomer and other Renaissance writers. Mae

Left: James Weldon Johnson, Carl Van Vechten portrait. *Library of Congress Prints and Photographs Division, Digital ID van 5a52189.*

Right: Bessie Smith. *Wikimedia Commons.*

West, another White habitué of the Harlem nightlife scene, often rubbed shoulders with Van Vechten.

Van Vechten and Marinoff, a Russian-born dancer and actress, had what can best be described as a modern marriage. In their spacious midtown apartment, they had their own bedrooms and maintained discreet private lives. He took male lovers, both White and Black, to an uptown pied-à-terre; she went on extended trips, for both professional and personal reasons. According the music journalist Chris Albertson, "Carlo," as many knew him, "had a weakness for [Harlem's] strapping young men."[176]

Sometimes the best of intentions can go awry, especially when there is a clash of cultures between downtown White society and uptown Black folk. A most revealing episode took place on the night of April 12, 1928, at a Van Vechten soirée. After his many attempts to lure Bessie Smith to his get-togethers, she finally gave in due to the prompting of one of her band members, Porter Grainger. According to her biographer, Smith "exquisitely sang 'six or seven numbers' taking a strong drink between each number"; according to Van Vechten, she sang three songs.

Fania Marinoff, Carl Van Vechten portrait. *Courtesy of the Library of Congress.*

Having to quickly leave in order to make a performance uptown at the Lafayette Theater, Smith and her group were making their way out of the apartment when Marinoff put her arms around her neck and declared, "Miss Smith, you're not leaving without kissing me goodbye." Smith, who had no problem with homoerotic encounters and was (in Van Vechten's word) "soused," screamed, "Get the fuck away from me." Pushing past Marinoff and knocking her to the floor in the process, Smith shouted, "I ain't never heard of such shit!" Attempting to rescue a major social catastrophe, Van Vechten whispered, "It's all right, Miss Smith, you were magnificent tonight." According to Van Vechten's biographer, Bruce Kellner, "the incident, laced with verbal obscenities, was elaborated on and passed around in Harlem until it took on mythic proportions, thereafter reported inaccurately."[177]

Van Vechten's Harlem hideaway was painted black with silver stars decorating the ceiling and red lights, giving the apartment a distinct pink glow. Jimmy Daniels, a famous African American song stylist who had a long-term affair with the architect Philip Johnson, once visited Van Vechten's Harlem lair. "It was a seductive place," he fondly recalled. "there were no chairs or tables, just red velvet cushions, and some of them were more like beds—well, I guess they *were* beds. It was a decorator's nightmare, and Carlo acted quite differently when he was there. I don't think Fania [Marinoff] even knew about the place."[178] Among Van Vechten's reported male lovers were the playwright Avery Hopwood, actor and designer Donald Angus and literary publicist Mark Lutz, with whom he had a ten-year affair. Van Vechten once described himself as "unpredictable, undependable, and inefficient, an atheistic opportunist with a hankering for liquor and a variety of odd ideas about sex."[179]

Van Vechten was also an indefatigable drinker, making the rounds of the midtown wet zone and uptown speakeasies almost every night. In midtown, he regularly dropped in at one of Texas's clubs as well as Tony's, popular with the Algonquin Round Table gang. However, it was in Harlem that he found his rhythm. He was a regular at Connie's Inn, the Cotton Club, the Lennox Avenue Club, Smalls Paradise and the Sugar Cane Club. He also visited less celebrated establishments like the Catagonia Club (aka Pod's and Jerry's), the Nest, Chez Florence, Club Ebony, Sheik Club, Leroy's, the Log Cabin, Lulu Belle, Smalls' New World and the Clam House.

GAY METROPOLIS

One of the most notorious venues for homoerotic assignations during the World War I era was the Lafayette Baths, located on Lafayette Street just south of Cooper Square in what is today's New York's East Village. The Lafayette was one of a handful of bathhouses that catered to an exclusively gay male—and mostly White—clientele, providing a safe environment for sexual encounters as well as other forms of socializing. The city sported still other baths that catered to a mixed male heterosexual-homosexual clientele and tolerated discreet sexual encounters. However, what distinguishes the Lafayette from the other popular bathhouses is that on December 29, 1916, the Gershwin family took over its ownership and Ira Gershwin became its manager.[180]

Throughout New York and other cities during Prohibition, men and, more infrequently, women appropriated a variety of social spaces to facilitate homoerotic liaisons. Encounters took place in the privacy of an apartment or rented hotel room; in the civic space of public parks, deserted streets, docks, beaches or tenement basements, stairwells and rooftops; in the quasi-public venues of bathhouses, a saloon's backroom, movie theaters, public toilets, washrooms and comfort stations (in other words, tearooms); and at social gatherings and invitation-only parties. One could say that illicit—if not illegal—sex was taking place nearly anywhere homosexuals could discreetly meet.[181]

Bathhouses like the Lafayette were a very different, yet equally unique, sexual venue, one that neither Van Vechten nor Texas seem to have ever visited. As Chauncey most perceptively notes, bathhouses "constituted a singular gay environment."[182] First and foremost, men came to meet other men for two purposes. They came to fulfill explicitly physical and sexual desires, to have sex, and they came to meet and socialize with other homosexual men. And when they met, they were either nude or modestly clothed, making explicit what under most public conditions would have remained concealed. Equally critical for this male population, these discreet settings allowed them to feel relatively safe from public harassment or police arrest.

According to Chauncey, "Gay baths were few in number and served a more limited—and generally more affluent—clientele than most of the other spaces gay men appropriated in the early twentieth century."[183] In addition to the Lafayette, other gay baths of the era were the Ariston Baths on West 55th Street, the Everard on West 28th Street, the Mount

Morris Baths at Madison Avenue at 125th Street, the Penn Post Baths on West 31st Street, the Produce Exchange Baths at 6 Broadway and the St. Mark's Bath on St. Mark's Place near 3rd Avenue. Among the gay-tolerant baths were the YMCA, the Claridge and Stauch's on Stillwell Avenue near Coney Island, Brooklyn.[184]

As one might expect, the men who visited bathhouses engaged in a range of sexual acts, including fellatio and sodomy. Some seemed to have participated in more radical forms of engagement—group and "public" sex. An undercover investigator witnessed a series of encounters at the Ariston Bathhouse. Over a two-hour period, two dozen men meandered in and out of the partially illuminated dormitory and cooling rooms. As Chauncey acknowledges, "Voyeurism and exhibitionism were an important part of the sexual excitement in the resulting light and shadow." As the observant investigator reported, while couples engaged in a variety of sex acts against a wall or lying on a nearby cot only a few feet away from him, other men stood and watched attentively.[185] Bathhouses constituted a unique sexual setting.

As the irony of history would have it, these baths grew out a half-century-long movement of socially minded progressive reformers seeking to better the life of immigrants and the poor. Given the poor quality of sanitary conditions and limited in-apartment toilets and baths, New York—like many municipalities during the late nineteenth and early twentieth centuries—built sex-segregated public baths to meet people's needs. Contemporaneous to this effort, local ethnic, fraternal and religious organizations as well as commercial entities set up similar bathing facilities. In time, some of these operations catered to a decidedly gay constituency.

Drawing the social function from their origins, as Chauncey astutely recognizes, "the baths were also important social centers, where gay men could meet openly, discuss their lives, and build a circle of friends." What makes this venue so important is that it was—and still is—an explicitly sexual terrain of social engagement. Not unlike traditional heterosexual brothels catering to all manner of illicit sexual indulgence, bathhouses were a unique cultural venue of self-expression, the experience of pleasure and the forging of community. There, as Chauncy notes, men "created a social world on the basis of a shared and marginalized sexuality."[186]

10
GANGLAND CITY

A Night on the Town

It was a hot Friday night in mid-July 1929, and three low-level waterfront hoods were out for a good time, speakeasy hopping from one wet zone joint to the next. It was late, and the toughs—the Cassidy brothers, Peter and William "Red," along with their buddy Simon "Sammy" Walker—were toasted. They wanted one more round before calling it a night. Stumbling down Broadway, they stopped at 1721 between 54th and 55th Streets, making the fateful mistake of going into the Hotsy Totsy Club & Grill.

This speak was, as a regular reported, "a dump," but a dive with a well-stocked bar. Once they passed the peephole test and were admitted, patrons walked down a dark hallway to get to a front room that measured only twelve by twenty feet and was jammed with a few small tables and chairs and, to the side, a piano and bandstand. That night, like most nights, Jerky Benson was jamming on the piano with a few backup musicians, and he was often joined by one of the club's two singing waiters, Harry Delson, a wet zone regular. A couple of hostesses with the reputation of being "morally loose," plied the tables. None got a salary, working only for tips. While the club had been running since 1924 and was repeatedly raided, the illegal hooch was safely hidden behind sliding wall panels. It was reported that this neighborhood hangout brought in between $2,000 and $4,000 a night.[187]

Arnold Rothstein. *Courtesy of the Library of Congress.*

The three small-time hard cases, tipsy and likely showing off for the hostesses, insulted and roughed up some of the employees. Sadly, they didn't know that the small roly-poly guy who ran the place was Hymie Cohen or that his partner was Jack "Legs" Diamond. Diamond and his sidekick and enforcer, Charles Entratta (aka Charles Green) and "Tough" George Heaghney were holding forth at the bar. An argument broke out over a welterweight fight earlier that night in which Ruby Goldstein, the "East Side Jewel," knocked out Billy Drako in the second round; Goldstein had stopped by the Hotsy earlier that night for a couple of celebratory rounds.

No one messed with Legs, especially in his speak. A fight broke out, and when the smoke cleared, Red Cassidy and Walker were dead and Peter Cassidy critically wounded. Some claim that Diamond told the waterfront boys to cool it, they gave him lip and the confrontation escalated into a brawl. As the tension mounted, Cohen had the band play "Alexander's Ragtime Band" as loud as possible. To this musical accompaniment, Diamond shot Red Cassidy twice, adding two more shots to the head for good luck, and Entratta plugged "Red" Walker.

John Thomas "Legs" Diamond was often called the "Clay Pigeon of the Underworld" because he survived at least five shootouts; he was one of Prohibition's legendary gangsters. Some called him New York's Al Capone.

Others saw him as a sociopath, a crazy killer. He got his start as gang boss Arnold Rothstein's bodyguard and soon defined Gotham's speakeasy scene. He was imbued with a reckless sense of immediacy and a fearless impulse to live for the moment, a reckless sensibility that gave the '20s its edge. Stanley Walker, a speakeasy habitué, described Legs as "a frail, tubercular little rat, cunning and cruel."[188] He was a smart dresser, carried lots of cash and was always out for a good time, especially at his Hotsy Totsy. More so, he liked to have a few drinks and, although married, fool around with "his girls," the hostesses. It is also said that the club had a private backroom where Legs used to whack some of his competitors and those who crossed him.

When the police arrived, no one but Hotsy Totsy employees and the dead and wounded remained; the twenty-five patrons, along with Legs and Entratta, had vanished. Police inspector Edward Mulroney took charge of the crime scene and, knowing that the Hotsy was Diamond's speak, put the gangster at the top of the suspect list. As the police started their investigation, witnesses suddenly began to turn up dead. First, the bodies of the bartender, William Wolgant, and three patrons, were found shot. Then came the bodies of the club's cashier, Thomas Ribler; the hat check girl, Gracie Carroll; and a waiter were found dead. Finally, Cohen disappeared, never to be seen or heard from again. Only one witness, Thomas Merola, a singing waiter, survived, but he hid out under police protective custody. When formally questioned, he insisted that he knew nothing: "I was dozing on the bandstand....I didn't see anything. I didn't hear anything, either."[189]

Now, with all witnesses taken care of, Legs and Entratta reappeared, insisting on their innocence. The police dropped the charges against them for lack of evidence. Such was the underbelly of New York's speakeasy scene.

RESPECTABLE CRIME

Illegal alcohol juiced the Roaring Twenties, and as the decade played out, more and more New Yorkers repudiated the Eighteenth Amendment to enjoy their favorite cocktail. In Gotham and most major cities, gangsters underwrote popular nightlife and the speakeasy scene, becoming national celebrities, overseers of all things illegal and illicit. Chicago's "Scarface" Capone was the era's most celebrated crime boss, achieving legendary status as the subject of endless newspaper and newsreel stories and, in time, dozens of books, movies and TV shows. Gotham's gangsters were less mythic figures, they were rather transformative characters who bridged the old-world ethnic gang and the new-world crime syndicate. Legs Diamond, Larry Fay, Owney Madden, Frank Costello, Barron Wilkins, Dutch Schultz, Frankie Uale (or Yale), Johnny Torrio, Lucky Luciano, Meyer Lansky and, most importantly, Arnold Rothstein, are among the best-known gangsters who called the Big Apple home. Coppola's Godfather series is the saga of the twentieth-century immigrant experience, a tale chronicling two generations in the life of a New York family who, through crime, achieve the American dream. Their experience is representative of the city's, and the nation's, ethnic immigrant minorities undergoing upward mobility, cultural integration and the dubious achievement of respectability.

The shootout at the Hotsy Totsy speak took place a few months before the great 1929 stock market crash. Both pointed to deeper systemic failings that slowly came to overwhelm the nation. The former symbolized the unraveling of the underground marketplace, the glue that kept illicit passions in check; the latter represented the collapse of the legitimate aboveground economy. Together, and building in parallel over years, these developments contributed to the socioeconomic crisis that changed America forever. The once-modest worlds of bootlegging crime and financial speculation were transformed by the exuberant prosperity of the '20s. The enormous expansion in consumer spending fermented the bubble economies of alcohol-fueled speakeasy indulgence and stock market run-ups that culminated in the '29 crash and the subsequent Great Depression.

Left: Gopher Gang—Owney Madden, back row, middle, leaning forward, circa 1910. *Wikimedia Commons.*

Right: Owen ("Owney") Vincent Madden, New York City Police Department mug shot (1931). *Library of Congress Control Number 2003680203.*

The underworld gang has been an established fixture of old New York since the mid-nineteenth century, replete with monikers like Dead Rabbits, Five Points Gang, Hudson Dusters and Gophers. Key innovations of twentieth-century technology, most notably the automobile, the telephone and the Thompson machine gun, industrialized crime and transformed the gang.[190] Flush with hitherto unimaginable mountains of cash generated from the wet trade, crime and the gangster were remade. At the start of Prohibition, gangsters worked for legitimate businessmen with vested interests in the alcohol trade; by the time of repeal in '33, everyone worked for the gang boss. In the process, gangsters expanded their operations into a growing array of both legitimate and illegal businesses, including nightclubs, restaurants, hotels, laundries and carting companies, forcefully taking over unions, running gambling and prostitution rackets and selling marijuana, cocaine and heroin.

As the capital of the twentieth century, Gotham was not going to be a prisoner to the premodern morals that temperance advocates sought to impose. Resistance came from a variety of quarters, each with its own rationale for breaking the law and each growing larger from year to year. One important group included East Side Bluebloods, fun-loving businessmen (those Guinan called "butter and egg men") and the bohemian and literary set that rejected the values of rural rubes and simply snubbed their collective nose at Prohibition's indignity.

A second group consisted of ethnic, working-class and poor citizenry, often Catholic and Jewish, who felt singled-out and discriminated against by the very White Protestant temperance movement. It included German, Irish, Italian and eastern European immigrants; African American migrants from the South; and a small but steadily growing Puerto Rican minority who became citizens following the passage of the 1916 Jones Act and others from the Caribbean.

Resistance also came from newly empowered young adults, college students and workers, many war veterans and working girls, the legendary flapper, who experienced Prohibition as an insult to their personal sense of freedom. They liked to smoke, dance, flirt and drink at their favorite speak. As Prohibition slowly unraveled during the '20s, opposition emerged from an unlikely group, the previous nondrinker who unexpectedly took up the bottle. They not only turned to the speak to join the party of illicit, inebriated fun, but also became fierce advocates for Prohibition's repeal. Still other opposition to Prohibition came from those with a vested interest in the alcohol trade and the most to lose by its suppression; they also had the most to gain from undermining its enforcement. This group included brewers and distillers; nightclub, cabaret and saloon owners; and restaurant and hotel operators, as well as the innumerable skilled craftsmen, drivers, tradesmen, wait staff and performers who kept the system running.

Fierce opposition came from politicians, especially those tied to the Tammany machine, whose Big Apple electoral constituency opposed Prohibition, as well as the New York police and Prohibition agents who benefited from the generous kickbacks that came their way. Finally, opposition came from gangsters and others who kept the network of distilleries, transportation, distribution and sales humming. Clearly, a sizeable number of New Yorkers rejected Prohibition and were welcomed into their favorite speak as if it was their second home.

The One and Owney

Texas Guinan's wet zone speak, the El Fey Club, and Harlem's most glamorous nightspot, the Cotton Club, had two things in common—they both offered illegal liquor and were both backed by Owney Madden. The grand chronicler of Gotham's underworld, Herbert Asbury, author of *The Gangs of New York*, on which Martin Scorsese's 2002 movie is based, left a vivid, if romanticized, vision of Madden: "He was sleek, slim and dapper, with the gentle smile of a cherub and the cunning and cruelty of a devil."[191] Owney was a graduate of Hell's Kitchen's Gopher gang and New York State's finest school of criminal higher education, Sing Sing penitentiary. He was often referred to as "Owney the Killer," a moniker he detested. Some hypothesize that he was the model for F. Scott Fitzgerald's Prohibition-era character Jay Gatsby.[192]

Owen "Owney" Victor Madden arrived in New York in 1902 at the age of eleven from Liverpool (some say Leeds), England, settling into the notorious West Side Irish ghetto Hell's Kitchen. As a teen, he was recruited into the Gophers (pronounced "Goofers"), and when it split into three factions a few years later, he got control of the West Side turf below 42nd Street. Owney was a gangster with at least nine lives. In November 1912, while attending a party at the Arbor Dance Hall on 52nd Street near 7th Avenue, he settled into a comfortable spot in the club's balcony only to be approached by eleven thugs from a rival gang, the Hudson Dusters. Surrounding him, they pulled their guns and plugged him with six shots. Remarkably, he survived.

Later, when questioned by the police in the hospital, Madden refused to identify the shooters—he had his own idea of justice. While Madden recuperated in the hospital, a low-level thug, William Moore (aka Little Patsy Doyle), who may have been one the shooters and is rumored to have been furious over rumors that Owney had tried to pick up his girlfriend, Freda Horner, attempted to take over Madden's turf. The first thing Owney did when released from the hospital was to set up Doyle's killing in a Hell's Kitchen saloon. Arrested and convicted, Madden was sentenced to ten to twenty years at Sing Sing.[193]

Following his release from Sing Sing in 1923, Madden became, in Walker's words, "the most important man in New York…the Elder Statesman, the Grand Old Man, of the rackets." Walker reports that "he looked and acted precisely as a racketeer should look and act." Madden was now lean and tough, a "catlike gentleman, with a falcon's profile, slicked-back black hair and blue eyes," eyes that Walker recalls vividly as "a very bright and piercing blue."[194] Madden looked like a Hollywood movie star gangster—and he acted like one.

Prohibition made Madden very rich. He controlled a major chunk of the city's illegal alcohol distribution and reportedly underwrote a number of the city's swankiest nightspots, including Guinan's many clubs as well as the Cotton Club, the Stork Club, the Silver Slipper, Duffy's Tavern and the Central Park Casino. Owney also financed a host of legitimate enterprises, including a laundry and a brewery and had a part interest in the boxing heavyweigh Primo Carnera. His Phoenix Cereal Beverage Company on West 26th Street was famous for its "Madden's No. 1," a beer that Walker fondly recalled as "a fine brew."[195]

Walker found Madden to be a typical New York gangster: "crafty, cruel, bold and lazy." Nothing better captures Owney's character—and the mounting crisis of the Roaring Twenties crime scene—than his 1932 confrontation with Vincent "Mad Dog" Coll. Coll, whom Walker calls "a stupid, reckless killer," was a protégé of Dutch Schultz, hit man and petty thug. Coll figured the best way to gain stature in Gotham's tough underworld was by kidnapping and ransoming members of the Madden mob, Dutch's principal rival. His first attempt to grab Owney's brother-in-law, John Marrin, failed. He then went after Owney's partner, George "Big Frenchy" DeMange, playing one of the oldest cons in the gangster's playbook—and it worked. Coll used fake cops to pick up Big Frenchy and demanded $20,000 for his unharmed release; Madden paid, but so did Coll.

Vincent "Mad Dog" Coll. *Wikimedia Commons.*

A couple of days after the incident, Coll called Owney from a telephone booth in a pharmacy at 8th Avenue and 23rd Street, taunting him about the kidnapping. Unbeknownst to Coll, a big black limo driven by Abraham "Bo" Weinberg pulled up outside the drugstore, and two of Madden's hit men, Leonard Scarnici and Anthony Fabrizzo, got out and entered the store, pulled Tommy guns from under their coats and ended Coll's career.

In the wake of the Coll murder, pressure mounted against Madden. He couldn't be tied to killing, so he was charged with a parole violation and sent back to Sing Sing. After release, he faced intensified gangland competition in the wake of the Depression and the repeal of Prohibition. He relocated to Hot Springs, Arkansas, in 1935 and opened the Hotel Arkansas, a popular spa and casino among the East Coast underworld, which operated for decade. Owney died in Hot Springs of natural causes in 1965.

Graft

During Prohibition, New York was an open city, and graft lubricated civil society. More rewarding than shaking down illegal alcohol purveyors was selling it ripe. Vice was seen as the gravest moral issue, and cops regularly visited houses of prostitution for money or sexual services or both. Cops occasionally got a little more imaginative, as evidenced by the "doctor's office racket," an example of a widespread extortion scam. A police plant entered a doctor's office when the doctor was out, complained to the nurse about a made-up illness, put cash in a conspicuous place and pulled down his pants; at this point, the police entered the office and threatened the nurse with arrest for prostitution if she didn't pay a bribe. Sometimes, but especially in Harlem, cops would simply break into someone's apartment threatening that if the resident didn't fork over some money they would arrest those present. This scheme proved quite lucrative on Saturday nights, when house parties often took place.

Not all cops or federal agents were on the take. The most colorful Prohibition agents were the daring duo of Isidor Einstein and Moe E. Smith, better known to the press and public as Izzy and Moe. When Prohibition took effect, Izzy was a postal clerk and Moe ran a cigar store. They had become friends through the Masons, and while neither had previous law enforcement experience, they thought being G-men would

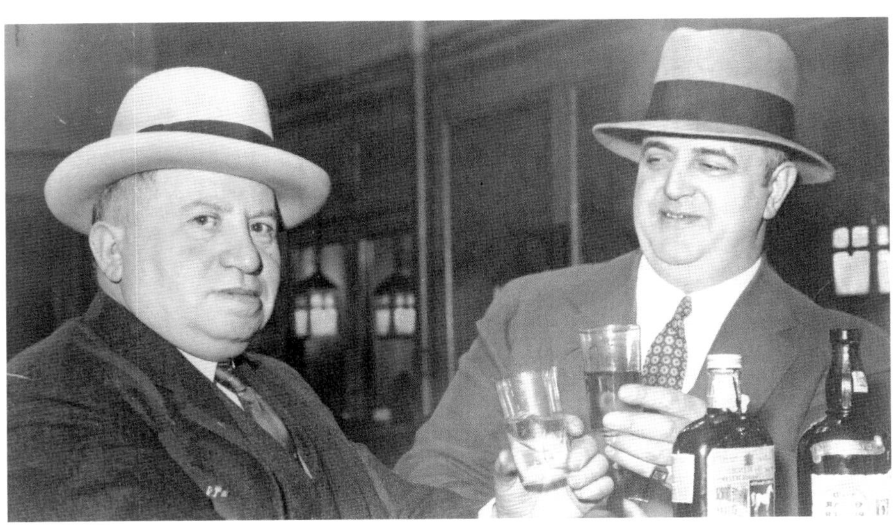

Isidor Einstein and Moe E. Smith (aka Izzy and Moe). *Wikimedia Commons.*

be exciting. They looked like the most unlikely agents, with Izzy standing only five feet, five inches and weighing 225 pounds, with Moe his Sancho Panza. They gained nationwide notoriety because Izzy spoke half a dozen European languages and took on an infinite array of ethnic disguises. He posed as a Jewish rabbi and a French maître d', an Italian fruit vendor and a German pickle packer, a Polish count and a Chinese launderer, a Texas cattleman and even an African American Harlem resident. The duo worked the city speaks for five years and are credited with confiscating five million bottles of liquor and making nearly five thousand arrests—they had a 95 percent conviction rate.[196]

Sadly, temptation abounded, and few federal or city law enforcement officials had the high moral standards of Izzy and Moe. Gambling was a lucrative illegal business that invited innumerable shakedowns. It included everything from customary card games, dice, roulette, pool and the slots to horse and dog races; sports pools for baseball, football and boxing; and numbers or "bird cage" lotteries. Howard McLellan, a '20s researcher, estimated that the gambling rackets throughout the country generated more than $4 billion annually ($59 billion in 2020 dollars) in illegal gain. He also found betting parlors operated in neighborhood pool halls, cigar stores and the back rooms of speakeasies.[197]

George S. Schuyler, a Harlem Renaissance writer, observed that gambling was so rampant uptown that "the chief pastime of Harlem seems to be playing the numbers." And gambling was one activity in which Tammany, the police and local gangsters scratched one another's backs. Rothstein, the fixer, got his start working for Tammany boss Timothy "Big Tim" Sullivan and he progressed up the rackets, he always loyally kicked back a percentage of his take to the Tammany machine. For this loyalty, Rothstein's gaming parlors were never raided. Similarly, Madden had deep ties to the West Side Tammany organization.

A corrupt police force and judiciary can include creative public servants. According to one account, the proprietor of a city speak estimated that he paid $1,370 per month to run his business, of which about 10 percent was paid to corrupt law officials, including federal agents, local cops and county district attorneys. This proprietor got a bargain compared to the tariffs imposed on not only other speakeasy operators but also many businesses, legal and not, operating in New York. Within the illegal alcohol trade, cops extorted money from not only speakeasy operators but also distillers, drivers, the retail vendors who sold the hooch and sometimes even patrons caught in a raid. The street cop's take was split with higher-ups in the police force, local politicians and the Tammany machine as well. The fix was in deep.

Cops were the foot soldiers of the "honest graft" extortion food chain, often functioning as middlemen or bagmen for the shakedown rackets orchestrated by Tammany hacks and/or Tammany-backed city officials. According to Herbert Mitgang, Tammany went after legitimate businesses in nearly every sector of the city's economy. Payoffs were demanded from florists, funeral parlor owners, furriers, garment manufacturers, kosher butchers, launderers, master barbers, milliners, paper box manufacturers, window cleaners and even wholesalers at the Fulton Fish Market.[198] Graft was but one more excess of the Roaring Twenties.

The Tammany corruption phenomenon reached its climax during the administration of New York's good-time mayor Jimmy Walker. He was elected mayor in 1926, the high point of the bubble decade. Walker was a charismatic politician who embodied the 1920s wild, fictitious exuberance. He was a true son of Tammany, for his father was a district leader. He worked his way up the ranks of the Tammany machine, serving in the state assembly and senate before becoming mayor. Looking more like a movie star than politician, he was often featured in page-one newspaper headlines accompanied by a sexy young starlet to the latest Broadway opening, political fundraiser or one of Guinan's speaks. Often called New York's "Night Time Mayor," Walker joked quite seriously that his trusted assistant was the daytime mayor. A married Catholic, he antagonized the church and respectable society with his very public affair with the actress Betty Compton.[199]

Corruption sometimes leads to its own negation. Under William "Boss" Tweed (1823–1878), payoffs and kickbacks were a modest added tax, accepted as a cost of doing business in the Gotham. By the time Walker took office, Tammany had elevated corruption, influence peddling and an infinite variety of rackets into get-rich schemes that were a way of life for greedy machine hacks. Against a background of a flush consumer marketplace and dysfunctional Prohibition enforcement, graft oiled civil society. However, as the decade wore on, corruption became increasingly abrasive, alienating many it supposedly served.

Tammany had long been opposed by the city's respectable establishment, especially the Protestant gentry and the *New York Times*. They railed against its corruption and political influence peddling, particularly its appeal to the city's vast ethnic minorities. However, in the wake of former governor Al Smith's failed presidential bid against Herbert Hoover in 1928 and the 1929 stock market crash, opposition to Tammany mounted. The shakedown was getting too expensive.

The state's new governor, Franklin D. Roosevelt, took office on January 1, 1929, and had no ties to the Tammany machine. In opposition to Smith, who owed his governorship to the machine, FDR saw Tammany as a potential liability to his great ambition of first securing the 1932 Democratic Party nomination and then winning the presidency. In an effort to represent himself as a "clean government" progressive, Roosevelt backed Judge Samuel Seabury's investigations into municipal corruption. Seabury's hearings led to page-one revelations about the enormous scale of malfeasance deforming the city's business. Most shocking was the staggering number of under-the-table payoffs that found their way into the hidden pockets of politicians, city officials, corrupt cops and Tammany bosses, often one and the same. Judge Seabury's campaign culminated with Walker's resignation from office in September 1932 and his embarking on a slow boat to Europe to avoid prosecution. As Walker's ocean liner ploughed across the Atlantic towards his luxurious retirement, the Hootse Tootsie was shuttered and abandoned, its night of blood-stained violence becoming just one more dark memory of the Prohibition era.

Will Magear "Boss" Tweed (1870). *Wikimedia Commons.*

11
PARTY'S OVER

Beginning of the End

Herbert Hoover took office as the thirty-first president on March 4, 1929, as the federal Prohibition campaign was failing. In a report to the Senate, the Treasury Department claimed that nine hundred Prohibition agents had been dismissed for lack of funds and various offenses. It argued that although 170,000 stills had been closed since Prohibition was established, this represented only 10 percent of total operating throughout the country. More troubling, it estimated that five to ten million gallons of hooch was smuggled into the country and that twenty million Americans were producing homebrew moonshine, including wine, cheap whiskey, bathtub gin and other concoctions.[200]

During the summer of '29, it was reported that there was a growing backlog of business inventories along with a decline in manufacturing output and the drop in wholesale prices. Innumerable farms were failing and in foreclosure. As the New Year commenced, the first of numerous Depression-era bank runs took place. Treasury Secretary Andrew Mellon sought to reassure the nation, proclaiming that the market must take its course and the Hoover administration would not intervene. As he famously pronounced, "Liquidate labor, liquidate stocks, liquidate real estate…values will be adjusted, and enterprising people will pick up the wreck from less-competent people."[201] By 1932, ten thousand banks had failed; the nation was reeling with nearly a quarter of the workforce unemployed and falling personal income. The October crash not only wiped out the American economy but also crushed the American spirit.

The Depression took a particular toll on Gotham. In April 1929, New York's police commissioner, Grover Whalen, estimated that there were thirty-two thousand speaks operating in the city.[202] By '32, half of the city's factories were closed, a third of the city's workforce was unemployed and those on relief topped 1.5 million. With no money in the male wage earner's pocket, domestic violence, evictions and family abandonments skyrocketed. The situation was particularly grim in Harlem, where the unemployment rate topped 50 percent.[203]

Gotham, like cities around the country, sprouted Hoovervilles, homeless encampments. In New York, a dozen or so were in Central Park and dubbed "Hoover Valley," "Shanty Town," "Squatters Village," "Forgotten Men's Gulch" and "Rockside Inn."[204] Other Manhattan encampments included "Hardlucksville," the city's largest encampment, at 10th Street on the East River, and "Camp Thomas Paine" in Riverside Park and the West 70s. Farther uptown, the homeless found residence in floating shanties

Hooverville huts and unemployed in West Houston and Mercer Street by Berenice Abbott in Manhattan, 1935. *New York Public Library Digital Collections catalog ID b13668355.*

along the Harlem River around 207th Street; at Camp Dyckman, which consisted mostly of World War I veterans; and at Marble Hill, just across the Spuyten Duyvil, where Sarah J. Atwood and her daughter, Mavis, ran a boxcar village.[205] The outer boroughs were also home to encampments. In Brooklyn, a large facility operated on Columbia Street, in Red Hook, and near today's Cadman Plaza in Brooklyn Heights, some six hundred people lived in "Hoover City." Writer Edward Newhouse lived for three weeks in a Queens encampment to do research for his novel *You Can't Live Here*.[206]

No place carried the scars of the pre-Depression frivolity of the Roaring Twenties more than the Broadway wet zone. No better Broadway habitué than Stanley Walker was shocked by the decline in the quality of midtown nightlife as the Depression deepened. He noted that "once there were lobster-palaces and cabarets now it cut-rate." He was most alarmed by the "cheap dances, lewd burlesque, filthy pictures…the hallmarks of the New Broadway."[207] Where once elegant speaks welcomed the society set, penny-a-dance "closed joints" became popular. As Walker lamented, "Many places for a while let their girls take off their dresses and cavort in rompers on special nights." And the number of "official" speaks declined to 9,000, significantly below the estimated 100,000 in 1925.[208]

THE BEGINNING OF THE END

As the story goes, Pauline Sabin's initial idea to form a national women's organization to oppose Prohibition took root at a 1928 congressional hearing. WCTU president Ella Boole, one of the nation's leading prohibitionists, proclaimed, "I represent the women of America!" Sabin recalled thinking to herself, "Well, lady, here's one woman you don't represent." And there were many, many more who felt the same way.

On March 7, 1929, three days after Republican Herbert Hoover's inauguration as America's thirty-first president, Sabin resigned as New York's Republican national committeewoman. She was the wife of Charles Hamilton Sabin, chairman of the board of the Guaranty Trust Company and treasurer of the Association Against the Prohibition Amendment (AAPA). "I want to devote my untrammeled efforts toward working for a change in the Prohibition law," she informed the party and the nation.[209] Shortly thereafter, Sabin welcomed a small group of New York's finest society women to her exclusive residence at No. 1 Sutton Place South.

Pauline Sabin. *Courtesy of the Library of Congress.*

Money and class privilege may buy political party allegiance, but they do not guarantee loyalty. Sabin, the steadfast Republican, campaigned for Hoover in his battle against the wet candidate, New York governor Al Smith. She was, however, deeply disappointed by his inauguration speech that proclaimed his continuing support for Prohibition:

> *No greater national service can be given by men and women of good will—who, I know, are not unmindful of the responsibilities of citizenship—than that they should, by their example, assist in stamping out crime and outlawry by refusing participation in and condemning all transactions with illegal liquor. Our whole system of self-government will crumble either if officials elect what laws they will enforce or citizens elect what laws they will support.*[210]

Sabin felt that Hoover broke a promise to convene a federal commission to assess Prohibition's failures and not to strengthen its enforcement procedures.

Two months later, on May 28, 1929, Sabin gathered fifty socially prominent women from seventeen states at Chicago's elegant Drake Hotel to form the Women's Organization for National Prohibition Reform (WONPR). Its mission was to challenge the abstinence establishment that included the president, Congress, state legislatures and women's temperance groups throughout the country. As the historian Caryn Neumann points out, "The creation of WONPR challenged the image of respectable women as enemies of beer, wine and liquor."[211] Sabin was named chairman.

As the '20s unraveled, Sabin found Prohibition's failings increasingly unacceptable. She knew firsthand the hypocrisy about alcohol consumption common among politicians and the gentry. Accustomed to martinis and dining in formality, she often hosted gatherings of society leaders at her home or attended such events at the homes of other women within her caste. At these soirees, many denounced the evils of alcohol—especially consumed by the city's poor and immigrant populations—while enjoying their favorite cocktails. She was disturbed by the growing power of bootleggers, the corruption of the police and politicians, and the erosion of national values. She feared the toll alcoholism was having on families and the young. Most troubling, she opposed the collusion of church and state in imposing moral order.

Sabin believed in temperance but opposed Prohibition because, as the preceding decade had shown, it did not work. America was being literally flooded by liquor and Americans were drinking at historically unprecedented levels. Enforcement of the Eighteenth Amendment was a failure, and it had to be repealed. In the place of prohibition, Sabin advocated regulation. She understood that neither church nor state could stop people from drinking. More so, she opposed the reach of the federal government into the control of personal individual life. She insisted that the government should not tell "citizens what they must or must not due in their strictly personal conduct as long as public safety is not affected, is not a function which the Government should not attempt."[212] She believed that a local government, be it the state or town, should determine who could legally sell alcohol, the level of the alcohol content, who could purchase it and at what price. Local regulation would restrict alcohol consumption; it would be more effective than federal legislation of abstinence in reducing—but not eliminating—drinking. Sabin introduced the modern public policy of the regulation of illicit intoxicants to American political life.[213]

Party's Over

The beginning of the end of Gotham's speakeasy party took place in July '29 when the shootout took place at the Hotsy Totsy Club run by Legs Diamond. Two thugs were found dead and one wounded in the speak, and mysteriously, all but one of the witnesses either died or disappeared, suggesting that there was no end to underworld violence. (On December 18, 1931, after being acquitted for the kidnapping and torture of a cider hauler in Troy, New York, Diamond was shot and killed in his hotel room.)[214]

The Hotsy Totsy shooting was but one of a growing number of showdowns scaring the tightening gangland economy. By 1931, the city's murder rate reached about 1,500, more than double the 712 in '21.[215] However, the July 28, 1931, shooting of five-year-old Michael Vengalli captured the attention of all New Yorkers and people around the country. The boy was playing with friends near the Helmar Social Club, operated by the Dutch Schultz mob, on East 107th Street close to 3rd Avenue. According to *Time*, "A touring car swung around the corner of Second Avenue. In the car were six men. They aimed shotguns and automatics in the general direction of a loafer lounging in front of the Helmar Club, opened fire." Vengalli was shot in the thigh, but the bullet penetrated his spine; he died later that day. Four other children were wounded, including Michael's seven-year-old brother, Salvatore, who was hit with five bullets.

The shootings created a firestorm of anger and recrimination. Governor Roosevelt voiced the concerns of many when he said, "I can express righteous indignation, but that won't help catch them." Mayor Walker and other politicians shared his outrage. City newspapers and the police offered rewards, and even the American Legion got into the act, offering to mobilize thirty thousand vigilantes to fight gangsters. Vincent "Mad Dog" Coll was eventually arrested for the killing; in December 1931, he was put on trial but was acquitted.[216]

Roosevelt, a reluctant "wet" Democrat, won the 1932 presidential election and was inaugurated before an audience of 150,000 on the bitter cold afternoon of March 4, 1933. In his speech, FDR proclaimed, "This great Nation will endure as it has endured, will revive and will prosper." Prohibition, temperance and the evils of alcohol were never mentioned. In nine months, the Eighteenth Amendment was inauspiciously repealed, and Prohibition ended.

As the Depression deepened, anti-Prohibition forces argued that continuing the temperance policy only intensified the nation's economic crisis. They noted that it had destroyed the brewing and distilling industries, causing the loss of millions of jobs. The policy contributed to the mounting agricultural depression with huge loses in grain production that would have supplied the brewers. Third, the federal government was spending millions of dollars annually in its effort to enforce a failed policy. Finally, they repeatedly pointed out that the government lost millions of dollars in tax revenues.[217]

The anti-Prohibition forces were divided into two tendencies. One consisted of those who favored outright repeal of the Eighteenth Amendment and a return of temperance regulation, if at all, to individual states. The second tendency believed it was impossible to overturn a constitutional amendment and, therefore called for nullification or modification of the Volstead Act by changing the definition of intoxication, thus permitting light wine and 3.2 percent beer. While many among the anti-Prohibition forces surely must have imbibed either in the privacy of their home or partied at a local speak, no one encouraged their fellow citizens to break the law of the land.

Roosevelt's role in Prohibition is the most critical and most curious. Andrew Sinclair points out that "the Roosevelt and Delano families belonged to the squire-archy of upper New York State."[218] As a Democrat among the rural gentry, the future president cautiously backed temperance. As an upstate politician, he opposed big-city Democrats, and especially the city's Tammany machine, who were strongly in favor of repeal. Perhaps more significant, his mother, Sara, and wife, Eleanor, were teetotalers. As governor, he kept the executive mansion dry but is reported to have regularly visited the home of his confidant and speechwriter Samuel Rosenman in Wappingers Falls for a cocktail or two.[219]

As the '32 Democratic campaign was waged, Roosevelt played a cat-and-mouse game over Prohibition. The more progressive Democrats, led by former New York governor Smith, advocated complete repeal; Roosevelt held to a moderate position, seeking a compromise by arguing for state's rights. As the story goes, "Roosevelt withdrew by telephone his opposition to Smith's minority wet plank some fifteen minutes before Smith was due to present it from the [Democratic Party] convention floor."[220] Like much of his subsequent New Deal legislation, Roosevelt's stand on Prohibition followed popular opinion and did not lead it. He was a marvelous political swimmer, able to keep his head above water as he was forcefully pushed forward by a more progressive tide.

In February 1933, the U.S. Congress passed a resolution for a new constitutional amendment to end Prohibition. Over the next eleven months, the required thirty-six states ratified what became the twenty-first amendment repealing the Eighteenth Amendment. During the afternoon of December 5, 1933, and as momentum for repeal mounted, President Roosevelt reminded his fellow Americans that "the objective we seek through a national policy is the education of every citizen toward a greater temperance throughout the nation."[221] At 5:32 p.m. Eastern Time, when Mormon-dominated Utah approved the amendment, few took his words to heart.

In short order, alcohol was again flowing through the city's streets. Even department stores got into the act. In Manhattan, Macy's boasted that it would not be undersold, offering name brands like Golden Wedding whiskey, Hennessy, Holloway's gin and Mumm's Cordon Rouge 1926 champagne. In Brooklyn, Abraham & Straus sold Johnny Walker Black Label.[222] When alcohol finally flowed freely, bootleggers became legitimate distributors, blind pigs became reputable local taverns and upscale watering holes again became fashionable supper-clubs. A new yet old era returned to American social life, but one shadowed by a deepening Depression that no amount of booze could hide.

Last Laugh

In 1925, Larry Fay convicted Texas that the grass was greener in Florida, and they traveled to Miami to open the Miami Del Fey. A local realter offered her a deal she couldn't refuse—yet she did. "Listen, sucker," she supposedly said, "you take them by the sun, I take them by the moon. Now don't let's interfere with each other's business." However, as the Miami land boom burst, the wet zone night owls fled back to the city and Tex split with Fay as her business partner.[223]

For Texas, 1929 started out as just another year of the speakeasy hustle. With her brother Tommy, she took over Club Intyme on West 54th Street, only to have city authorities reject the club's license application. Nevertheless, on April 19, the police closed down Club Intyme and arrested six employees (including a Chinese cook) for selling food without a license. Texas's attorney, Maxwell Lopin, secured a reversal and the club reopened. A week later, City Marshal Michael Kennedy again closed down the club, famously saying, "I'm probably the last sucker to step in here....I am going to give the little girl a great big hand." City officials then seized all the club's furnishings.

As the Gotham nightlife scene tightened, Texas defended speakeasies against increased federal raids. She insisted that "about 150 persons depend upon my club for a livelihood...seventy-five entertainers and waiters and as many taxi drivers....These dependents will be forced out of work, and this will complicate the city's unemployment problem."[224] She sought out new opportunities, including a short-lived roadhouse in Valley Stream, Long Island.

In December of '29, Texas and her troupe of Guinan Graduates went to Chicago to perform at the Green Valley Cabaret. However, in the early hours of March 23, 1930, a shootout at the club between the managers and the property owner ended her stay in the Windy City. She returned to Gotham and reopened the 300 Club, this time as the Argonaut. On October 29, the Argonaut was raided, as an officer reported, "while gayety was at its height and Miss Guinan was urging 200 guests to 'give her little girls a big hand.'" The police seized a handful of bottles filled with ginger ale and champagne.

During this period, Guinan kept up her public presence. Paramount Famous Lasky Corporation invited her to appear in the musical revue *Glorifying the American Girl*, supervised by Florenz Ziegfeld; it was released on December 7, 1929, and included Rudy Vallée, Helen Morgan, Eddie Cantor, and Jimmy and Mrs. Walker. Texas also spoke at a town hall meeting of the National Woman's Party on May 18, 1930, considering the Mastick law that limited the women's workweek to forty-eight hours. Women objected to the New York law because no comparable law was proposed for men. Guinan called for a test case of the law, arguing, "Why, we could swamp the politicians who refuse to assist us, if we combined our vote in the proper way!"[225]

In 1930, Tex was invited to perform in France and traveled with her troupe of thirty aboard the French liner *Paris*. She was first barred from landing in England for being a reputed criminal. Upon arrival in Le Havre on May 20, she was forced to remain on board and then stay at the less-than-fashionable Hotel Transatlantique, described as "a 'bunkhouse' for third-class emigrants." After a monthlong standoff, the French government refused her entry, and she was forced to return to New York. Arriving back in Gotham on June 9 at the West 50th Street pier. She lamented, "I was a sucker to come 3,000 miles to go to jail when every jail in America is waiting for me....But you know—an indiscretion a day keeps depression away."

After a short stint in a nightclub show, *Too Hot for Paris*, at Bayes Theatre, she launched a transcontinental bus tour to promote the show accompanied by forty-six performers. On September 19, hundreds gathered at Broadway and 49th Street to wish her and her troupe farewell. She joked, "This trip is an anti-depression tour....My company will donate a portion of its earnings in each city to local unemployment relief." Not surprising, the tour was banned in numerous small towns and cities; the mayor of Waltham, Massachusetts, announced, "If the show's too hot for Paris, it's too hot for Waltham."

While on her tour, she announced plans to marry her latest beau, Mortimer Davis Jr., a Montreal theater manager; it was never consummated. In September 1933, she rode her horse, Pieface, in the Pasadena, California Labor Day parade with Tom Mix and others. She took time out of her West Coast tour to perform in Darryl Zanuck's 20th Century company production, *Broadway Thru a Keyhole*, a story written by her old friend, Walter Winchell; it opened on November 1 at the Rivoli Theatre. While performing in the Northwest, Texas complained about intestinal pains and was diagnosed with amoebic dysentery. On November 4, in a Vancouver hospital, she underwent surgery and died—just a month before Prohibition was repealed.

Texas Guinan (with necklace). *Billy Rose Theatre Division, The New York Public Library Digital Collections, Shelf locator: *T PHO A.*

Texas Guinan's funeral was held at Campbells Funeral Church, on Broadway between 66th and 67th Streets, and some 12,000 people viewed her body. The *Times* reported, "Miss Guinan's body was dressed in a while chiffon sequin gown—she had been partial to sequins." It added: "In her left hand was a rosary and upon her third finger a large diamond. Another diamond of comparable size was upon the little finger of her right hand. Around her neck was a diamond pendent. Part of the silver-colored bronze coffin was covered with orchids." Over 7,500 people gathered for her burial.

As Stein reported in his unpublished biography of Guinan, the girl from Texas reflected wistfully on her life, "Better a square foot of New York than all the rest of the world in a lump—better a lamppost on Broadway than the brightest star in the sky."[226]

Conclusion

TWENTY-FIRST-CENTURY PROHIBITION

Prohibition Failed

Texas Guinan died on November 5, 1933, one month before Prohibition was repealed on December 5. She died at age forty-nine, no longer the Broadway showgirl, cowgirl movie star or Queen of the Speakeasies that had propelled her career for three decades. Had she not gotten sick and died in Vancouver and returned to Gotham, she would have faced a far, far different city than the one she knew so well. The Great Depression was deepening, and people—even the "suckers" she adored—no longer had the play money for the fun and frivolity nightclubs offered during the Roaring Twenties. How she would have fared in this new Gotham is anyone's guess.

Prohibition failed, and as of this writing, the Eighteenth is the only amendment to be repealed. There were two fundamental developments that resulted from Prohibition and its repeal. First, the old-fashioned gangs of the '20s morphed into organized crime syndicates that rule today's underworld. Second, four years after the Eighteenth Amendment was repealed and Prohibition ended, Congress adopted the Marihuana Tax Act on August 2, 1937. It made the possession and sale of marijuana illegal.

Half a century later, Nancy Reagan launched the postmodern prohibition movement. In 1982, while attending a gathering at the predominately Black Longfellow Elementary School in Oakland, California, a student asked what she would do if offered illegal drugs, to which she replied, "Just say

No." Mrs. Reagan's original campaign sought to address an assortment of alleged youthful vices, including alcohol and drug abuse, peer violence and premarital sex. Seeing an opportunity, a cabal of shrewd moralists, clever politicians and innovative entrepreneurs used the speech to formally launch the nation's war on drugs.

Jeffrey Miron and Katherine Waldock, two academic analysts, estimate that legalizing currently illegal drugs would save Americans approximately $41 billion a year in federal and state government expenditures relating to drug enforcement.[227] In the three decades since Mrs. Reagan uttered her dubious words of warning, the total costs of the war on drugs is estimated at $1 trillion.

The war on drugs has proved as successful as the original campaign against alcohol. Both were failures. In the nine decades since Prohibition was repealed, comparable "wars" to suppress still other transgressive activities have proved far less then successful. These include wars on gambling, pornography and "consensual" adult sex work as well as battles against race mixing, erotic music and dance, abortion and homosexuality. These diverse issues have defined the culture wars that continue to divide American politics and social life.

"War" on Transgression

The regulation of alcohol takes place at the state and/or local level where people buy and consume alcoholic beverages. At this level, a hodgepodge of diverse and often incompatible statutes is in force. Throughout the country, there are localities that still remain "dry," prohibiting the sale of alcoholic beverages. Most states adhere to some form of traditional Blue Laws restricting the sale of alcoholic beverages on Sunday, whether covering all day or for designed hours, to honor religious traditions. States also determine the minimum age for alcohol consumption (often twenty-one years) and the age of those who can sell alcohol at on-premises and off-premises establishments, whether a bar or liquor store (often eighteen years).

In 1937, just four years after Prohibition was repealed, Congress passed the Marihuana Tax Act (in the 1930s, marijuana was spelled "marihuana"). During the 1930s, hemp was popular and profitable, used for a variety of commercial purposes, including the smoking kind. The act sought to garner the federal government much needed tax revenues without outlawing marijuana production or consumption. In 1970, President Richard Nixon championed the Controlled Substances Act superseding the Marihuana Act and launched the war on drugs—a decade before Mrs. Reagan's speech. In the decades since the adoption of the Marihuana Act and the programs promoted by President Nixon and Mrs. Reagan, the war on drugs has dragged on. As of 2020, marijuana is legal for medical purposes in thirty-three states and for recreational purposes in eleven states and Washington, D.C.[228]

As marijuana consumption has been normalized, gambling and commercial sex have been mainstreamed. Gambling, one of the well-established rackets of Prohibition-era gangsters, has become a major commercial enterprise. In 1976, the federal Commission on the Review of National Policy toward Gambling recognized that gaming, like alcohol consumption, "is inevitable. No matter what is said or done by advocates or opponents of gambling in all its various forms, it is an activity that is practiced, or tacitly endorsed, by a substantial majority of Americans."[229] Such activities include state lotteries for every conceivable hustle; pari-mutuel betting on horses, greyhounds and jai-alai; sports bookmaking for every sport, from ping-pong to the Olympics; card games, keno and bingo; slot machines; and video poker, blackjack and roulette machines. Casinos revenues were nearly $42 billion in 2018.[230] In 2018, the Supreme Court ruled in *Murphy v. NCAA* that sports betting is legal. The rackets are big business; Al Capone and Owney Madden must be spinning in their graves.

Gambling might be a victimless crime; commercial sex is not. As the old adage states, prostitution is the oldest profession, and sadly, it is still alive and well in the twenty-first century. Sex work is a contradiction: morally, sex work is a sin because no one should sell their sexual being; socially, under capitalism, sex—the human body—is a commodity and people sell their sexual selves to survive.

Since the nation's founding, women (and sometimes men) have been selling their sexual labor for what is perceived to have value, be it money, food, trinkets or social opportunities. Today, commercial sex is regulated in only one state, Nevada, and restricted to mostly rural areas. Not surprising, prostitution takes place throughout the country and operates under various names. Streetwalkers persist but are relegated to the poorest exchanges. Ever innovative, prostitution has long adapted to the latest technology. In the 1920s, the telephone refashioned the bordello into the call house. A century later, the digital revolution is helping to mainstream commercial sex work. In addition, commercial sex is also facilitated through massage parlors and gentlemen's or strip clubs. The dark side of prostitution is the recruitment of young girls (and some boys) and the forced sex slavery (in other words, trafficking) of foreign women that characterizes much of the commercial sex throughout the world.

Anthony Comstock. *Wikimedia Commons.*

America's modern "war" against pornography began in 1873 with the passage of the Comstock Act, which barred obscene materials from the U.S. mail. Named after Anthony Comstock, it covered not only allegedly obscene or pornographic materials but also sex education pamphlets and birth control devices as well. An important crack in the Comstock Act occurred in 1936 when a federal appeals court ruled in *U.S. v. One Package of Japanese Pessaries* that doctors had the right to dispense contraceptives to their patients. This part of the Comstock Act was finally ended in 1965 with the Supreme Court ruling *Griswold v. Connecticut*, which ended the ban on sales of contraceptive devises to adults.

Ongoing battles over obscene or indecent materials continue, promoted by the widespread availability of risqué materials through cable television and the internet. Efforts to limit porn through the 1996 Communications Decency Act have been repeatedly rejected by the courts. Recent federal court decisions against the FCC relating to Janet Jackson's "costume malfunction" and Cher's and Nicole Richie's use of the "F word" put such regulation in question. However, one area of content suppression that continues to find widespread legal and popular support is the restriction of child pornography and the arrest of those caught either distributing or receiving such material.

Abortion and homosexuality, along with interracial sex and erotic music and dance, are very different kinds of "transgressions." They have each long been areas of bitter contestation, pitting moral conservatives and religious traditionalists against cultural secularist and political progressives. A combination of personal valor (in other words, a willingness to challenge accepted moral or social conventions) and market forces (or amoral cultural innovation) has redefined modern America cultural values. In essence, these wars, whether fought over alcohol consumption or the latest sexy fashion, mark the shifting boundaries of acceptable individual conduct.

SPEAKEASIES LIVE ON

Transgression has been integrated into postmodern American life. Once transgression signified either the illegal or the immoral; today, it is the risqué, the cutting-edge of acceptable indulgence. Other than acts of sexual terror, committed in rapes, sexual slavery or pedophilia, everything sexual between consenting adults is acceptable. Welcome to the twenty-first century's new normal.

A century ago, Prohibition transformed alcohol consumption from an immoral practice into an illegal act, fostering the speakeasy and the reconfiguration of American moral values. With the repeal of Prohibition, alcohol consumption became a regulated adult indulgence, illegal if it violated a local convention but nonetheless an all-American pleasure. The original Roaring Twenties speak was a unique, unprecedented innovation of American entrepreneurialism, an iconic expression of popular culture. During its short thirteen-year existence, it cultivated the full gamut of personal and social expressions that would come to define post–World War II life, let alone twenty-first-century postmodernity.

Since the country's founding four centuries ago, Americans have fought over what is acceptable moral conduct. Some have battled to preserve the traditional, to repress notions of radical erotic experience and expression; others have pushed the boundaries of acceptable pleasure. This battle continues, continually reshaped by history and changes in moral values. Today, the meaning of transgression is in flux, buffeted by differences between the legal and the popular notions of what is acceptable behavior.

America in 2020 is not what it was in 1920. The new woman of old is the everywoman of today; the New Negro is today's every American of color; the "pansy" of yesterday is just another person; the gangster persists along with the underground economy; and the cocktail continues to represent the radical sense of sensual pleasure that defines postmodern America.

During the '20s, the speakeasy was the nexus of social transgression. It fostered a host of subversive activities, from simply getting drunk at the bar to grand dinning, sensual dancing and listening to hot jazz to wild sexual experiences, both heterosexual and homosexual as well as interracial mingling. Prohibition incubated postmodern sexuality. During the '20s, the speak was the place to be.

With the end of Prohibition, the speakeasy and the world it facilitated disappeared. Nevertheless, transgression lived on, flourishing as part of the post–World War II consumer revolution. The '50s introduced Bettie

Page and the first gay leather bars. The 1960s counterculture revolution celebrated sex, drugs and rock-and-roll. Hippies got stoned, blissed out on music, LSD and the beginning of a new sex culture. In this early second-wave feminist age, patriarchal heterosexual sex clubs opened across the country, and *Playboy* became one the nation's most important publications. Since then, the Christian culture wars have fought to halt the integration of transgression into the market economy and its popular acceptance as normal. These wars have been only marginally successful, making American life evermore erotic.

Few today recall that *hipsters* originally meant those who carried an alcohol-filled flask during Prohibition. Speakeasies live on in twenty-first century New York. They include hideaways in Manhattan's Lower East Side like the Violet Hour, the Back Room and PDT (aka Please Don't Tell) and Rye in Brooklyn's Williamsburg. They are discreetly located on anonymous streets, often with no name or address on the door. They advertise: one can find them, and they offer nothing transgressive. Sadly, New York is no longer the speakeasy city. One can only wonder what Texas Guinan would make of it.

Appendix 1
TEXAS GUINAN SAYINGS

- "Better a square foot of New York than all the rest of the world in a lump—better a lamppost on Broadway than the brightest star in the sky."
- "Hello, sucker!"
- "Don't give a sucker a break!"
- "Butter and egg men."
- "Give the little lady a great big hand."
- "Remember he may be all the world to his mother, but he is just a cover charge to you."
- "Never let a fool kiss you and never let a kiss fool you."
- "Virtue pays—if you can find a market for it."
- "A wisecrack a day keeps depression away."
- "Home is a great place—after all the other places have closed."
- "A politician is a fellow who will lay down your life for his country."
- "Success has killed more men than bullets."
- "Marriage is all right, but I think it's carrying love a little bit too far."
- "He bought me so many orchids that I looked like a well-kept grave."
- "A guy who'd cheat on his wife would cheat at cards."
- "I like noise, rhinestone heels, plenty of attention, and a red velvet bathing suit. I smoke like a 5-alarm fire. I eat an aspirin every night before I got to bed. I call every man I don't know 'Fred' and they love it."

Appendix 2

GLIMPSES OF TEXAS GUINAN

- Texas as a cow girl (1900)
  https://www.youtube.com/watch?v=gWvopKEzXBw
- Texas stars in "White Squaw" (1920)
  https://www.youtube.com/watch?v=4Yb-sJojj4I
- Texas hosts a speakeasy (1928)
  https://www.youtube.com/watch?v=CSqk4m4W_3E
- Texas calls herself "sucker" on return to New York (1930)
  https://www.youtube.com/watch?v=oqhMxpNL5N8
- Texas introduces fan dancer Sally Rand (1931)
  https://www.youtube.com/watch?v=ObiUgeCGD9A

Appendix 3

GOTHAM SPEAKEASIES

*This list is intended to illustrate some, but not all, of the innumerable speaks that operated in Gotham during Prohibition.**

DOWNTOWN

55 Bar	55 Christopher Street
181 (Julius & Renganeschi)	181 West 10th Street
Barney Gallant's	85 West 3rd Street
Black Rabbit	MacDougal Street and Minetta Lane
The Blue Horse	21 East 8th Street
Chez Desert	53 West 24th Street
Chumley's	86 Bedford Street
Claudio's	on a waterfront pier
Club Dorame	149A West 13th Street
Club Gallant	40 Washington Square South and 85 West 3rd Street
Dukes	Division Street

* Due to space limitations, a fuller list of speaks could not be included.

Eve's Place (aka Hangout)	129 MacDougal Street
The Flower Pot	Christopher and Gay Streets
The Four Trees	1 Sheridan Square
Fronton	88 Washington Place
Gino's	14 Van Nest Place
Greenwich Village Inn	5 Sheridan Square; 47 West 3rd Street
Gypsy Tavern	64 Washington Square South
Jack's	88 Charles Street
John and Jean's	139 West 10th Street
Julian's	159 West 10th Street
Louis' Luncheon	116 MacDougal Street
Mario	140 West 13th Street
Maxim's	42 West 8th Street
The Nut Club	99 7th Avenue
O'Leary's	on the Bowery
The Old Club	139 West 10th Street
The Open Door	135 MacDougal Street
Paul and Joe's (original)	6th Avenue at 9th Street
The Pepper Pot	146 West 4th Street
The Pirate's Den	8 Christopher Street
The Red Head	West 8th Street
Red Mask	Charles Street
Sam's	MacDougal Street
Stonewall	91 7th Avenue
Tavern	7th Avenue South
Three Steps Down	West 8th Street
The Washington Square	19 Washington Square North

WET ZONE

48 East 53rd Street	
57 East 54th Street	
The 33 Club	48 East 53rd Street
The 44th Street Club	405 West 44th Street
The 50/50 Club	129 West 50th Street
The 300 Club (aka Arganout)	151 West 54th Street
Les Ambassadeurs Club	Broadway near 50th Street
Artists & Writers	215 West 40th Street
The Ascot Club	128 East 54th Street
The Astor	49th Street and Broadway
Back Stage Club	110 East 56th Street
Bath Club	35 West 53rd Street
Beaux Arts Café	West 40th Street
Biarritz 3	8 East 52nd Street
Bill's Gay Nineties	57 East 54th Street
Biltmore Cascades	43rd Street at Madison Avenue
Casa Blanca	33 West 56th Street
Chesterfield Inn	133 West 49th Street
Central Park Casio	Central Park
Chateau Bruno	6 West 53rd Street
Chez Morgan	West 54th Street
Chez Richard	110 East 61st Street
Club Alabam	216 West 44th Street
The Club Argonaut	151 West 54th Street
Club Durant	232 West 58th Street
Club Europa	310 West 58th Street
Club Ha-Ha	West 52nd Street
Club Intyme (aka"Intime")	Harding Hotel, 203–11 West 54th Street

Club Lido	806 7th Avenue
Club Napoleon	33 East 56th Street also home to Place Elegant, Mona Lisa, Petit Palais and the Europa
Club New Yorker	8 East 51st Street
Club Richelieu	West 51st Street
Club Richman	157 West 56th Street
Club Samoa	??
Colony Club	564 Park Avenue
Côte D'Azure Club	64 West 55th Street
Côte D'Or	41 East 50th Street
Country Club	East 58th Street
Dinty Moore's	West 46th Street
Dizzy Club (aka the Disney Club)	64 West 52nd Street; 146 East 56th Street
Don Juan	38 East 53rd Street.
L'Escargot D'Or	254 West 54th Street (penthouse)
The Everglades	203 West 48th Street
The Excelsior	149 East 56th Street
El Fey Club	123 West 45th Street
Famous Door	35 West 52nd Street
Les Fleurs	West 44th Street
The Furnace Club	131 West 52nd Street
Gold Room	??
Gus' (aka Gusses)	112 East 52nd Street
Gus & Eddie	338 East 43rd Street
Heigh-Ho Club	35 East 53rd Street
Hi Hat	150 East 56th Street
Hollywood Restaurant	Broadway at 48th Street (did not serve alcohol)
Hotel Ambassador	Park Avenue and 51st Street

Hotel Pennsylvania	33rd Street and 7th Avenue
Hotsy Totsy Club & Grill	1721 Broadway between 54th and 55th Streets
Hugo Pompeii Club	120 West 49th Street
The Hunt Club	122½ West 45th Street
Jack and Charlie's (later 21)	42 West 49th Street, later 21 West 52nd Street
Jimmy's	54 East 53rd Street
Jungle Bar (aka Ratner's Backroom)	120 Norfolk Street
The Kentucky Club	Broadway and 49th Street
King Cole Room (Knickerbocker Hotel)	Broadway and 42nd Street
Leon & Eddie's (L & E)	105 West 38th Street; 18 West 52nd Street
Louis & Armand's	46 East 53rd Street, then 42 East 52nd Street
Madison Square Men's Club	29 East 28th Street
Maison Royale	6 East 52nd Street
The Mansion	27 West 51st Street
Mona Lisa	36 West 56th Street;
New Mona Lisa 64	West 55th Street
Mulligan's Kitchen	422 East 55th Street
The New Ball and Chain	56 East 52nd Street
New Entre Nous	44 East 52nd Street
Old Fashion Club	50th Street, west of 6th Avenue
Paradise Restaurant	58th Street and 8th Avenue
Paramount Grill	46th Street and 8th Avenue
Park Central Casio	Central Park
Park View Club	54 East 53rd Street
Parody Club	West 48th Street
Pen & Pencil	205 East 45th Street
The Pent House	139 East 57th Street

Peter's Blue Hour	West 48th Street
Plunkett's	53rd Street west of Broadway
Porky Murray	West 52nd Street
The Place	in the 40s, off 6th Avenue
The Press Club	141 East 46th Street
The Press Grill	152 East 41st Street
The Puncheon Grotto	West 49th Street
Reymando	54 East 55th Street
The Roosevelt Grill	45th Street and Madison Avenue
The Roxy Grill	155 West 46th Street
The Royal Box	17 West 56th Street
Salon Royal	310 West 58th Street
Ship Ahoy	52 West 51st Street
Silver Ball	78 East 56th Street
Silver Room	384 Park Avenue
The Silver Slipper	201 West 48th Street
Simplon Club	26 West 53rd Street; formerly The European Club
Stork Club	152 West 58th Street, then New Stork Club 51½ East 51st Street, The Stork Rest, 51st Street at Park Avenue, after repeal, at 3 East 53rd Street
The Strollers	67 East 59th Street
Surf Club	2 East 52nd Street
T & N	50 West 52nd Street
Tap Room	52 West 58th Street
Texas Guinan Club	117 West 48th Street
Tony's (Tony Gardella)	42 East 53rd Street
Tony's (Tony Soma) (basement)	59 West 52nd Street
Le Touquet Club	37 West 53rd Street

The Villa Vallee	12 East 60th Street
The Wigwam Café	49th Street
The Wing Club	8 West 52nd Street
Zani's	37 East 50th Street
Zum Brauhau	239 East 86th Street

UPTOWN

Alamo Café	125th Street
The Bamboo	??
Basement Brown's	??
Bath Club	??
Book Store	134th Street (cellar club)
Broadway Jones's Supper Club	??
Breakfast Club	??
The Catagonia Club (aka Pod's & Jerry's)	166 West 133rd Street
Chez Florence	??
Clam House	146 West 133rd Street
Club Ebony	??
Club Pansy	??
Connie's Inn	131st Street and 7th Avenue
The Cotton Club	142nd Street and Lenox Avenue
Dickie Wells'	East 136th Street (or 133rd Street) and 7th Avenue
The Drool Inn	??
The Ebony Club	??
The Exclusive Club	102 West 136th Street
Garden of Joy (outdoor club)	7th Avenue between 138th and 139th Streets
Hole in the Wall	??

Johanny Jackson's	135th Street and 7th Avenue
The Lenox Avenue Club	43rd Street and Lenox Avenue
The Log Cabin	??
Lulu Belle Club	341 Lenox Avenue, near 127th Street
The Madhouse	169 West 133rd Street
Mexico	133rd Street
Mike's	7th Avenue in the 140s Streets
The Nest	169 West 133rd Street
The Plantation	West 126th Street
Saratoga Club	575 Lenox Avenue
Sheik Club	??
Smalls Paradise	136th Street and 7th Avenue
Smalls New World	??
The Spider Web	126th Street and 7th Avenue
Sugar Cane Club	??
Tabb's	140th Street and Lenox Avenue
Tillie's	148 West 133rd Street
Ubangi Club	??
Yeahman (Yeah Man)	135th Street and 7th Avenue
Zanzibar	??

The Boroughs

Adonis Social Club	154 20th Street, Brooklyn
The Boulevard	163rd Street, the Bronx
Harvard Inn	Coney Island, Brooklyn
Hermit's Inn	Broad Channel, Queens
The Hotel Bossert	Montague Street, Brooklyn
Hub Social Club	Brook Avenue, the Bronx
The St. George Hotel	Clark Street, Brooklyn

UNKNOWN LOCATION

Casanova	??
Cave of Fallen Angels	??
Texas Tommy	??

SPECIALTY SHOPS

(where one could purchase alcoholic products and their phone numbers)

Charlie Keep in Good Spirits	Wickersham 2-2313
F.A.D	Wickersham 2-4822
Happy Days Are Here Again	Circle 7-8966, 5974, 8974
John Kelly	Columbus 5-7429
Lloyd's	Vanderbilt 3-3240
Frank Murray	Plaza 3-3958
Frank's	Bryant 9-7116
Hudson Cordials (247 West 10th Street)	Chelsea 3-9179
Marcello	Wickesham 2-9055
McCan	Rector 2-7596
Ritz Cordial Shoppe (638 Lexington Avenue)	Vanderbilt 3-8161
George Roberts	Wickersham 2-2640
Standard	Wisconsin 7-6311
Henry Storm (209 East 14th Street)	Stuyvesant 9-8979
Tudor (71 Lexington Avenue)	Murray Hill 4-8748

NOTES

Epigraph

1. Berliner, *Texas Guinan*, 46.

Preface

2. Berliner, *Texas Guinan*. See also Walker, *Night Club Era*; Peretti, *Nightclub City*; Lerner, *Dry Manhattan*; and Okrent, *Last Call.*

Introduction

3. Walker, *Night Club Era*, 2, 4–8.
4. Erenberg, *Stepping Out*, 233.
5. Goddard, "Origin and Meaning of the Name," 283.
6. Morris, "US Alcohol Sales Increased"; NCSL, "State Medical Marijuana Laws"; Havocscope, "Prostitution Revenue Worldwide."
7. White, "World War I Played Key Role."
8. Gordon, *Second Coming of the KKK*, 95–96.
9. Aimone, "1918 Influenza Epidemic."
10. Hochschild, "When Americas Tried to Deport Radicals."
11. Jones, "Prohibition and Eugenics." See also Wilson, "Bad Habits and Bad Genes."

12. Walker, *Night Club Era*, 85–86.
13. Blum, "At the Prohibition Bar."
14. Benjamin, "Paris, Capital of the 19th Century."
15. Okrent, *Last Call*, 111.
16. Allen, *Horrible Prettiness*, 72; Felten, "Drink's French Connection,"; Sanford, "Illegal Alcohol Traffic," 43.
17. Ostandler, "Revolution of Morals," 339.
18. Latham, *Posing a Threat*, 21.
19. Peiss, *Hope in a Jar*, 55.
20. Ostandler, "Revolution of Morals," 330.
21. Chauncey, *Gay New York*, 310.
22. Leonard, *Mae West*, 53.
23. Berliner, *Texas Guinan*, 13.
24. Stein and Grace, "Hello Sucker," 3.
25. Ibid., 109.
26. Ibid., 3.

Chapter 1. Party Time

27. Ibid., 109–10.
28. Ibid., 110–13; Berliner, *Texas Guinan*, 94–95.
29. Stein and Grace, "Hello Sucker," 169.
30. Walker, *Night Club Era*, 244.
31. Shirley, *Hello, Sucker*, 48.
32. Stein and Grace, "Hello Sucker," 105, 144; Berliner, *Texas Guinan*, 108; Leonard, *Mae West*, q-13.
33. Stein and Grace, "Hello Sucker," 140.
34. Ibid., 140–42.
35. Caldwell, *New York Nights*, 228; Inflation Calculator, www.in2013dollars.com.
36. Bubbeo, *Women of Warner Brothers*, 104–5.
37. Stein and Grace, "Hello Sucker," 171–74.
38. Ibid., 169, 178–80.
39. "New Plays in Manhattan," *Time*, July 1927.
40. Walker, *Night Club Era*, 66.
41. Stein and Grace, "Hello Sucker," 213; Berliner, *Texas Guinan*, 132.
42. Walsh, *Gentleman Jimmy Walker*, 187–88; Stein and Grace, "Hello Sucker," 251.

Chapter 2. Speakeasy City

43. Hirschfeld, *Hirschfeld's Harlem*, 4.
44. Grauer, "Speakeasies I Remember."
45. drinkfocus.com.
46. Museum of the American Cocktail, "Origin of the Cocktail."
47. *Wall Street Journal*, October 6, 2007.
48. Murdock, *Domesticating Drinking*, q-105.
49. Hirschfeld and Kahn, *Speakeasies of 1932*, 22.
50. Internet Movie Database, "Donnie Brasco."
51. Asbury, *Great Illusion*, 211.
52. Drinking Cup, "Speakeasies and Blind Pigs."
53. Morris, *Wait Until Dark*, 113–20.
54. Ibid., 116, 120, 122.
55. Ibid., q115.
56. Ibid., 112.
57. Ibid., 125–33.
58. Ibid., q/122.
59. Norris, "Your Essay in Extermination."
60. Lerner, *Dry Manhattan*, 180.
61. Lender and Martin, *Drinking in America*, 258.
62. Thornton, *Economics of Prohibition*, 101–7.
63. Miron and Zwiebel, "Economic Case against Drug Prohibition."
64. Warburton, *Economic Results of Prohibition*.
65. Miller, "We Want Beer."
66. Thornton, "Alcohol Prohibition Was a Failure"; Blum, "At the Prohibition Bar."
67. Lender and Martin, *Drinking in America*, 138; Thornton, "Alcohol Prohibition Was a Failure."
68. Hirschfeld, *Speakeasies of 1932*, 70.

Chapter 3. From Cowgirl to Showgirl

69. Berliner, *Texas Guinan*, 4–11.
70. Shirley, *Hello, Sucker*, 3.
71. Berliner, *Texas Guinan*, 10.
72. Ibid., 21.
73. Ibid, 37; Shirley, *Hello, Sucker*, 4-5.
74. Berliner, *Texas Guinan*, 40.
75. Ibid., 46–48, 50, 55–56.
76. Ibid., 50.

77. Ibid., 61
78. Ibid., 64–69.
79. Shirley, *Hello, Sucker*, 17–18.
80. Berliner, *Texas Guinan*, 39.
81. Shirley, *Hello, Sucker*, 40.
82. Stein and Grace, "Hello Sucker," 98–100.
83. Shirley, *Hello, Sucker*, 44.
84. Berliner, *Texas Guinan*, 85, 214–15.

Chapter 4. Party Time in the Wet Zone

85. Eberly, *Music in the Air*, 42
86. Grimes, *Appetite City*, 232–35.
87. Okrent, *Last Call*, 208.
88. Hirschfeld, *Speakeasies of 1932*, 24.
89. measuringworth.com.
90. 21club.com.
91. Blumenthal, *Stork Club*, 87.
92. Erenberg, *Stepping Out*, 236–38.
93. Ibid., 189.
94. Walker, *Night Club Era*, 139; Caldwell, *New York Nights*, 242–46.

Chapter 5. Party Time Downtown

95. Stein and Grace, "Hello Sucker," 122.
96. Walker, *Night Club Era*, 280.
97. Watson, *Strange Bedfellows*, 137–38.
98. Huggins, *Harlem Renaissance*, 99.
99. Barnet, *All-Night Party*, 43–44.
100. Chauncey, *Gay New York*, 243–44.
101. Walker, *Night Club Era*, 236.
102. Ware, *Greenwich Village*, 58.
103. Ibid., 53.
104. Ibid., 58.
105. Walker, *Night Club Era*, 294–95.
106. Chauncey, *Gay New York*, 240, 242.

Chapter 6. Party Time Uptown

107. Okrent, *Last Call*, 212.

108. Osofsky, *Harlem*, 22.
109. Ibid., 35.
110. Ibid., 184.
111. Walker, *Night Club Era*, 101.
112. Ellington, "Nights at the Cotton Club,"
113. Jablonski, *Harold Arlen*, 45.
114. Teachout, *Pops*, 135.
115. Walker, *Night Club Era*, 94.
116. Anderson, *This Was Harlem*, 170–71.
117. Ottley, *New World A-Coming*, 48.
118. Hughes, "The Cat and the Saxophone (2 a.m.)."
119. Thurman, *Negro Life in New York*, 27.
120. Jones and Jones, *Willie Suicide Jones*.
121. Anderson, *Harlem*, 170.
122. King, *Whose Harlem Is This*, 140.
123. Ottley, *New World A-Coming*, 49.
124. Ibid., 64.
125. Wilson, *Bulldaggers, Pansies and Chocolate Babies*, 19.
126. Smith and Hoefer, *Music on My Mind*.

Chapter 7. Party Time in the Other Gotham

127. Demographia, "City of New York & Boroughs Population."
128. montesnyc.com
129. NYFood Museum, "Beer.".
130. "New York Speakeasies Under a New Attack," *Brooklyn Daily Eagle*, May 1, 1932.
131. Dalzell, "Whiskey Wars."
132. NYCEDC, "Raising a Glass."
133. Gustafson, "Brooklyn Army Terminal."
134. Geberer, "Opinion"; Gangster BB, "Christmas Day Massacre."
135. Marques, "Prohibition."
136. CUNY Academic Commons, "Bronx Was Brewing."
137. Conde, "Prohibition Began on This Day"; NY Facts You Ought to Know, "The Bronx."
138. Anderson, "Van Gogh's Ear II'"; Free Information Society, "Schultz, Dutch."
139. DeLong, "Gangster Dutch Schultz"; U.S. Dept of Labor, "CPI Inflation Calculator."
140. Queens Historical Society, "Queens History Timeline"; Thirteen/WNET, "Walk Through Queens."

141. Hofmann, "Originators of Rheingold Beer."
142. Broad Channel Historical Society, "Glimpse of the Past."
143. Old Timer, "How Prohibition Changed Ridgewood."

Chapter 8. Sex and Other Pleasures

144. Peretti, *Jazz in American Culture*, 44.
145. Garber, "Spectacle in Color," 322.
146. Woolner, "Famous Lady Lovers," 235.
147. Albertson, *Bessie*, 140.
148. Adler, *House Is Not a Home*, 73.
149. Hamilton, "*When I'm Bad, I'm Better*", 26.
150. Chauncey, *Gay New York*, 307.
151. Peretti, *Nightclub City*, 14.
152. Chauncey, *Gay New York*, 65.
153. Mumford, *Interzones*, 103.
154. Allen, *Horrible Prettiness*, 271.
155. Ibid., 230.
156. Ibid., 244.
157 Clement, *Love for Sale*, 179–80.
158 Allen, *Horrible Prettiness*, 236.
159. Ibid., 230.
160. Gertzman, *Bookleggers and Smuthounds*, 79.
161. Adler, *House Is Not a Home*, 34.

Chapter 9. Pansy City

162. Chauncey, *Gay New York*, 292.
163. Ibid.
164. Ibid., 310.
165. Wilson, *Bulldaggers, Pansies, and Chocolate Babies*, q-99.
166. Kamil and Wakin, *Big Onion Guide to New York City*, 101.
167. Wilson, *Bulldaggers, Pansies, and Chocolate Babies*, q-89.
168. Hughes, *Big Sea*, 273.
169. Wilson, *Bulldaggers, Pansies, and Chocolate Babies*, 109–10.
170. Walker, *Night Club Era*, 101.
171. Nugent, "On 'Gloria Swanson'," 211.
172. Smith and Hoefer, *Music on My Mind*, 159.
173. Johnson, "Go Down, Death"; Samuels, *Gift of Story*; this incident is not in Van Vechten's "Daybook" for June 1925; Van Vechten, *Splendid Drunken Twenties*, 87–90.

174. Coleman, *Carl Van Vechten*, 90–96.
175. Lueders, *Carl Van Vechten*, 116.
176. Albertson, *Bessie*, 139.
177. Lewis, *When Harlem Was in Vogue*, 183–84; Albertson, *Bessie*, 143–45; Van Vechten, *Keep A-inchin' Along*, 204.
178. Albertson, *Bessie*, 138.
179. Van Vechten, "My Friend: James Weldon Johnson," 24.
180. Chauncey, *Gay New York*, 221.
181. Ibid., 39–42, 185, 190, 195, 202 and 205; Faderman, *Odd Girls and Twilight Lovers*, 72–76; Peritti, *Nightclub City*, 119–23; Lapovsky Kennedy and Davis, *Boots of Leather*, 22–25.
182. Chauncey, *Gay New York*, 223.
183. Ibid.
184 Chauncey, *Gay New York*, 155, 210–11; see also Gustav-Wrathall, *Take the Young Stranger*, 158–69.
185. Chauncey, *Gay New York*, 212–14.
186. Ibid.

Chapter 10. Gangland City

187. Kofoel, "Hotsy Totsy Club."
188. Walker, *Night Club Era*, 234.
189. Sylvester, *No Cover Charge*, 13–20.
190. Sinclair, *Prohibition*, 220–41.
191. Asbury, *Gangs of New York*, 323.
192. Charyn, *Gangsters and Gold Diggers*, 75.
193. Asbury, *Gangs of New York*, 332.
194. Walker, *Night Club Era*, 103, 105, 106.
195. Ibid., 110.
196. Maeder, "Rumhounds Izzy Einstein and Moe Smith."
197. McLellan, "Now It's Gambling,"
198. Mitgang, *Once Upon a Time in New York*, 128.
199. Ibid., 220–24.

Chapter 11. Party's Over

200. Shirley, *Hello, Sucker*, 92–93.
201. Cannadine, *Mellon*, 445
202. Shirley, *Hello, Sucker*, 92–93.
203. Robertson, White, Garton and White, "This Harlem Life."

204. Jackson, Keller and Flood, *Encyclopedia of New York City*, 1063.
205. Thompson, "My Inwood."
206. Caldwell, *New York Nights*, 253–56.
207. Walker, *Night Club Era*, 203, 205.
208. Ibid., 208–9, 213.
209. *Time*, June 10, 1929.
210. Hoover, "Inaugural Address."
211. Neumann, "End of Gender Solidarity," 36.
212. Ibid., q-38.
213. Kyvig, *Repealing National Prohibition*, 471–72.
214. Walker, *Night Club Era*, 239.
215. Lerner, *Dry Manhattan*, 257.
216. *Time*, August 10, 1931
217. Sinclair, *Prohibition*, 371.
218. Ibid., 375.
219. Ibid., 376.
220. Ibid., 384.
221. "Prohibition Repeal Is Ratified at 5:32 P.M.," *New York Times*, December 5, 1933.
222. *Time*, December 18, 1933.
223. Trachtenberg, "Texas Guinan."
224. Shirley, *Hello, Sucker*, 95–100.
225. "Mastick Law Stirs Women's Protest," *New York Times*, May 19, 1930.
226. Berliner, *Texas Guinan*, 46.

Conclusion

227. Miron and Zwiebel, "Economic Case against Drug Prohibition."
228. Dodge, "Marijuana Legalization." See also Bennett, "Federal Drug War Spending."
229. U.S. Government Commission on the Review of National Policy toward Gambling, 1.
230. American Gaming Association, June 11, 2019.

BIBLIOGRAPHY

Adelman, Bob. *Tijuana Bibles: Art and Wit in America's Forbidden Funnies, 1930s–1950s*. New York: Simon & Schuster Editions, 1997.

Adler, Polly. *A House Is Not a Home*. New York: Rinehart & Company, 1953.

Aimone, Francesco. "The 1918 Influenza Epidemic in New York City: A Review of the Public Health Response." *Public Health Reports* 125, suppl. 3 (2010): 71–79.

Albertson, Chris. *Bessie*. New York: Stein & Day, 1972.

Allen, Robert C. *Horrible Prettiness: Burlesque and American Culture*. Chapel Hill: University of North Carolina Press, 1991.

American Gaming Association. "Commercial Casino Gaming Revenue Reaches $41.7 Billion in 2018, an All-Time High." June 11, 2019. americangaming.org.

Anderson, Darran. "Van Gogh's Ear II—the Last Words of Dutch Schulz." *3:AM Magazine: Whatever It Is, We're Against It*, February 11, 2019.

Anderson, Jervis. *Harlem: The Great Black Way, 1900–1950*. London: Orbis, 1982.

———. *This Was Harlem, 1900–1950*. New York: Farrar Straus Giroux, 1981.

Asbury, Herbert. *The Gangs of Chicago: An Informal History of the Chicago Underworld*. New York: Random House, 1986.

———. *The Gangs of New York: An Informal History of the Underworld*. New York: Thunder Mouth Press, 2003.

———. *The Great Illusion: An Informal History of Prohibition*. New York: Praeger, 1968.

Barnet, Andrea. *All-Night Party: The Women of Bohemian Greenwich Village and Harlem, 1913–1930*. Chapel Hill, NC: Algonquin Books, 2004.

Barr, Andrew. *Drink: A Social History of America*. New York: Carroll & Graf, 1999.

Benjamin, Walter. "Paris, Capital of the 19th Century." In *Illuminations: Essays & Reflections*. Edited by Hannah Arendt. New York: Houghton Mifflin Harcourt, 1968.

Bennett, Brian C. "Federal Drug War Spending vs Past Year Use Rates." ONDCP National Drug Control Strategy National Survey on Drug Use and Health, 2006. http://briancbennett.com/charts/fed-data/spending-vs-new-use.htm.

Benzon, William L. *Beethoven's Anvil: Music in Mind and Culture*. New York: Basic Books, 2001.

Berliner, Louise. *Texas Guinan: Queen of the Nightclubs*. Austin: University of Texas Press, 1993.

Blum, Deborah. "At the Prohibition Bar." *Wired*, December 31, 2018.

Blumenthal, Ralph. *Stork Club: America's Most Famous Nightspot and the Lost World of Cafe Society*. Boston: Little Brown, 2001.

Broad Channel Historical Society. "A Glimpse of the Past." www.broadchannelhistoricalsociety.org/glimpse.html

Bubbeo, Daniel. *The Women of Warner Brothers: The Lives and Careers of 15 Leading Ladies*. Jefferson, NC: McFarland & Company, 2002.

Burnham, J.D. "New Perspectives on the Prohibition 'Experiment' of the 1920s." *Journal of Social History* 2 (Fall 1968): 51–68.

Burrows, Edwin G., and Mike Wallace. *Gotham: A History of New York City to 1898*. New York: Oxford University Press, 1999.

Caldwell, Mark. *New York Nights: The Mystique and Its History*. New York: Scribner, 2005.

Cannadine, David. *Mellon: An American Life*. New York: Knopf, 2006.

Charyn, Jerome. *Gangsters and Gold Diggers: Old New York, the Jazz Age, and the Birth of Broadway*. Boston: Da Capo Press, 2004.

Chauncey, George. *Gay New York: Gender, Urban Culture, and the Making of the Gay Male World, 1890–1940*. New York: Basic Books, 1994.

Chevigny, Paul. *Gigs: Jazz and Cabaret Laws in New York City*. New York: Routledge, 1991.

Clark, Larry D. "'Can't Someone Find Him a Stimulant?' The Treatment of Prohibition on the American Stage, 1920–1933." *Theatre History Studies* (January 2009): 122–47.

Clement, Elizabeth. *Love for Sale: Courting, Treating, and Prostitution in New York City, 1900–1945*. Chapel Hill: University of North Carolina Press, 2006.

Cohen, Harvey G. *Duke Ellington's America*. Chicago: University of Chicago Press, 2010.

Coleman, Leon. *Carl Van Vechten and the Harlem Renaissance: A Critical Assessment*. New York: Garland Publishing, 1998.

Commission on the Review of National Policy toward Gambling, Final Report. Washington, D.C., 1976. https://babel.hathitrust.org/cgi/pt?id=osu.32435014750525&view=1up&seq=15.

Conde, Ed García. "Prohibition Began on This Day 95 Years Ago Impacting a Major Industry in the South Bronx." *Bronx Stories History*, January 16, 2015.

CUNY Academic Commons. "The Bronx Was Brewing: A Digital Resource of a Lost Industry." https://commons.gc.cuny.edu.

Dalzell, Rebecca. "The Whiskey Wars That Left Brooklyn in Ruins." *Smithsonian*, November 18, 2014.

DeLong, William. "Gangster Dutch Schultz Died a Millionaire, but Where Did All His Money Go?" *ATI*, March 30, 2018.

Demographia. "City of New York & Boroughs Population & Population Density from 1790." demographia.com.

Dodge, Blake. "Marijuana Legalization in 2020." *Newsweek*, December 27, 2019.

Douglas, Ann. *Terrible Honesty: Mongrel Manhattan in the 1920s*. New York: Noonday Press, 1995.

Drinking Cup. "Speakeasies and Blind Pigs: The Influence of the Illicit Prohibition Bar." drinkingcup.net.

Dunlop, M.H. *Gilded City: Scandal and Sensation in Turn-of-the-Century New York*. New York: William Morrow, 2000.

Eberly, Philip K. *Music in the Air: America's Changing Taste in Popular Music, 1920–1980*. New York: Hastings House, 1982.

Ellington, Edward Kennedy (Duke). *Music Is My Life*. New York: Doubleday, 1973.

———. "Nights at the Cotton Club." In *The Harlem Reader*, edited by Herb Boyd, 74–79. New York: Three River Press, 2003.

Erenberg, Lewis A. "From New York to Middletown: Repeal and the Legitimization of Nightlife in the Great Depression." *American Quarterly* 38, no. 5 (Winter 1986): 761–78.

———. *Stepping Out: New York Nightlife and the Transformation of American Culture, 1890–1930*. Chicago: University of Chicago Press, 1981.

Faderman, Lillian. *Odd Girls and Twilight Lovers: A History of Lesbian Life in Twentieth-Century America*. New York: Columbia University Press, 1991.

Fass, Paula S. *The Dames & the Beautiful: American Youth in the 1920s*. New York: Oxford University Press, 1977.

Felten, Erik. "A Drink's French Connection." *Wall Street Journal*, April 14, 2007.

Fisher, Irving, et al. "The Economics of Prohibition." *American Economic Review* Supplement 17 (March 1927): 5–10.

Fitzpatrick, Kevin C. *A Journey into Dorothy Parker's New York*. Berkeley, CA: Roaring Forties Press, 2005.

Forma, Warren. *They Were Ragtime*. New York: Grosset & Dunlop, 1976.

Free Information Society. "Schultz, Dutch." freeinfosociety.com.

Gangster BB. "Christmas Day Massacre 1920s," December 15, 2013. gangsterbb.net.

Garber, Eric. "A Spectacle in Color: The Lesbian and Gay Subculture of Jazz Age Harlem." In *Hidden from History: Reclaiming the Gay and Lesbian Past*, edited by Martin Bauml Duberman, Martha Vicinus and George Chauncey Jr., 318–31. New York: NAL Books, 1989.

Garber, Neil. *Winchell: Gossip, Power and the Culture of Celebrity*. New York: Knopf, 1995.

Geberer, Raanan. "OPINION: A Real Story of Prohibition in Brooklyn Heights." *Brooklyn Daily Eagle*, July 30, 2014.

Gertzman, Jay A. *Bookleggers and Smuthounds: The Trade in Erotica, 1920–1940*. Philadelphia: University of Pennsylvania, 1999.

Gilfoyle, Timothy J. *City of Eros: New York City, Prostitution, and the Commercialization of Sex, 1790–1920*. New York: Norton, 1992.

Goddard, Ives. "The Origin and Meaning of the Name 'Manhattan.'" *New York History* (Fall 2010): 277–93.

Goff, Brian, and Gary Anderson. "The Political Economy of Prohibition in the United States, 1919–1933." *Social Science Quarterly* 75 (June 1994): 270–83.

Gordon, Linda. *The Second Coming of the KKK: The Ku Klux Klan of the 1920s and American Political Tradition*. New York: W.W. Norton/Liveright, 2017.

Grauer, Neil A. "The Speakeasies I Remember; and Interview with Al Hirschfeld." *American Heritage* 54, no. 3 (June/July 2003).

Grimes, William. *Appetite City: A Culinary History of New York*. New York: North Point Press, 2009.

———. *Shake Up or On the Rocks: A Cultural History of American Drink*. New York: Simon & Schuster, 1993.

Gustafson, Andrew. "Brooklyn Army Terminal: Fortress of Prohibition," Turnstile Tours, August 28, 2013.

Gustav-Wrathall, John. *Take the Young Stranger by the Hand: Same-Sex Relations and the YMCA*. Chicago: University of Chicago Press, 1998.

Hamilton, Marybeth. *"When I'm Bad, I'm Better": Mae West, Sex, and American Entertainment*. Berkeley, University of California Press, 1997.

Havocscope Black Market. "Prostitution Revenue Worldwide." havocscope.com.

Hirschfeld, Al. *Hirschfeld's Harlem*. New York: Glenn Young Books, 2006.

Hirschfeld, Al, with Gordon Kahn. *The Speakeasies of 1932*. New York: Glenn Young Books, 2006.

Hochschild, Adam. "When Americas Tried to Deport Radicals." *New Yorker*, November 4, 2019.

Hofmann, Rolf. "The Originators of Rheingold Beer: From Ludwigsburg to Brooklyn—A Dynasty of German-Jewish Brewers." June 21, 2001. beerhistory.com.

Hoover, Herbert. "Inaugural Address," March 4, 1929. https://avalon.law.yale.edu/20th_century/hoover.asp.

Huggins, Nathan Irving. *Harlem Renaissance*. New York: Oxford University Press, 1971.

Hughes, Langston. *The Big Sea, An Autobiography*. New York: Hill & Wang, 1993.

———."The Cat and the Saxophone (2 a.m.)," 1926.

Jablonski, Edward. *Harold Arlen: Rhythm, Rainbows, and Blues*. Boston: Northeastern University Press, 1996

———. *Irving Berlin: American Troubadour.* New York: Henry Holt, 1999.

Jackson, Kenneth T., Lisa Keller and Nancy Flood. *The Encyclopedia of New York City*. New Haven. CT: Yale University Press, 1995.

James, Rian. *Dining in New York*. New York: John Day Company, 1931.

Johnson, James Weldon. "Go Down, Death." poets.org.

Jones, Bartlett C. "Prohibition and Eugenics, 1920–1933." *Journal of the History of Medicine and Allied Sciences* 18, no. 2 (April 1963): 158–73.

Jones, William S., and Kimberly D Jones. *Willie Suicide Jones: Falling from the Sky*. N.p.: Page Publishing, 2018.

Kamil, Seth I., and Eric Wakin. *The Big Onion Guide to New York City: Ten Historic Tours*. New York: New York University Press, 2002.

Kenney, William Howland. *Recorded Music in American Life: The Phonograph and Popular Memory, 1890–1945*. New York: Oxford University Press, 1999.

Kibler, M. Alison. *Rank Ladies: Gender and Cultural Hierarchy in American Vaudeville.* Chapel Hill: University of North Carolina Press, 1999.

King, Shannon. *Whose Harlem Is This, Anyway?: Community Politics and Grassroots Activism During the New Negro Era.* New York: New York University Press, 2015.

Kingsdale, Jon M. "The 'Poor-Man's Club': Social Functions of Urban Working-Class Saloon," *American Quarterly* 25, no. 4 (October 1973): 472–89.

Kisseloff, Jeff. *You Must Remember This: An Oral History of Manhattan from the 1980s to World War II*. Baltimore: Johns Hopkins University Press, 1989.

Kofoel, Jack. "Hotsy Totsy Club." *Miami News*, June 5, 1941.

Kyvig, David E. *Repealing National Prohibition*. Chicago: University of Chicago Press, 1979.

———. "Women Against Prohibition," *American Quarterly* 28, no. 4 (Autumn 1976): 465–82.

Lambert, Eddie. *A Listener's Guide to Duke Ellington*. New Brunswick, NJ: Rutgers University Press, 1999.

Langum, David J. *Crossing Over the Line: Legislating Morality and the Mann Act*. Chicago: University of Chicago Press, 1994.

Lapovsky Kennedy, Elizabeth, and Madeline Davis. *Boots of Leather, Slippers of Gold: A History of the Lesbian Community*. New York: Penguin Books, 1994.

Latham, Angela L. *Posing a Threat: Flappers, Chorus Girls, and Other Brazen Performers of the American 1920s*. Hanover, NH: Wesleyan University Press, 2000.

Lawrence, A.H. *Duke Ellington and His World: A Biography*. New York: Routledge, 2001.

Lender, Mark Edward, and James Kirby Martin. *Drinking in America: A History*. New York: Free Press, 1987.

Leonard, Maurice. *Mae West: Empress of Sex*. New York: Birch Line Press, Carroll Communications, 1991.

Lerner, Michael. *Dry Manhattan: Prohibition in New York City*. Cambridge, MA: Harvard University Press, 2007.

Levine, Lawrence W. *Highbrow/Lowbrow: The Emergence of Cultural Hierarchy in America*. Cambridge, MA: Harvard University Press, 1988.

Lewis, David Levering. *When Harlem Was in Vogue*. New York: Oxford University Press, 1981.

Long, Kay. *The Forbidden Apple: A Century of Sex and Sin in New York City*. New York: Ig Publishing, 2009.

Loughery, John. *The Other Side of Silence: Men's Lives and Gay Identities—A Twentieth-Century History*. New York: Henry Holt & Company, 1999.

Lueders, Edward. *Carl Van Vechten and the Twenties*. Albuquerque: University of New Mexico Press, 1955.

MacKellen, Landis. *The "Double Idemnity" Murder: Ruth Snyer, Judd Grey & New York's Crime of the Century*. Syracuse, NY: Syracuse University Press, 2006.

Maeder, Jay. "Rumhounds Izzy Einstein and Moe Smith Turned Prohibition Arrests into Comedy," *New York Daily News*, August 14, 2017.

Marques, Stuart. "Prohibition." NYC Department of Records & Information Services, March 8, 2019. https://www1.nyc.gov/site/records/index.page.

McLellan, Howard. "Now It's Gambling." *New York Herald Tribune Magazine*, December 13, 1933.

Miller, Carl. "We Want Beer: Prohibition and the Will To Imbibe—Part 1." Beer History, beerhistory.com.

Miron, Jeffrey, and Katherine Waldock. "The Budgetary Impact of Ending Drug Prohibition." Cato Institute, 2010. www.cato.org.

Miron, Jeffrey and Jeffrey Zwiebel. "The Economic Case against Drug Prohibition." *Journal of Economic Perspectives* 9, no. 4 (1995): 175–92.

Mitchell, Joseph. *Up in the Old Hotel and Other Stories.* New York: Random House, 1993.

Mitgang, Herbert. *Once Upon a Time in New York: Jimmy Walker, Franklin Roosevelt and the Last Great Battle of the Jazz Age.* New York: Free Press, 2000.

Mizejewski, Linda. *Ziegfeld Girl: Image and Icon in Culture and Cinema.* Durham, NC: Duke University Press, 1999.

Moore, Lucy. *Anything Goes: A Biography of the Twenties*. New York: Overlook Press, 2010.

Morris, Lloyd. *Incredible New York: High Life and Low Life of the Last Hundred Years*. New York: Random House, 1951.

Morris, Ronald. *Wait Until Dark: Jazz and the Underworld 1880–1949*. Bowling Green, OH: Bowling Green University Popular Press, 1980.

Morris, Seren. "US Alcohol Sales Increased by 5.1% in 2018." *Drinking Business*, January 17, 2019.

Mumford, Kevin. *Interzones: Black/White Sex Districts in Chicago and New York in the Early Twentieth Century*. New York: Columbia University Press, 1997.

Murdock, Catherine Gilbert. *Domesticating Drinking: Women, Men, and Alcohol in America, 1970–1940*. Baltimore: Johns Hopkins University Press, 1998.

Museum of the American Cocktail. "Origin of the Cocktail." www.kingcocktail.com/motac/museum/TheBalance.html.

Myers, Margaret. *A Financial History of the United States*. New York: Columbia University Press, 1970.

Nasaw, David. *Going Out: The Rise and Fall of Public Amusements*. New York: Basic Books, 1993.

National Conference of State Legislatures (NCSL). "State Medical Marijuana Laws." September 27, 2019. ncsl.org.

Neumann, Caryn E. "The End of Gender Solidarity: The History of the Women's Organization for National Prohibition Reform in the United States, 1929–1933." *Journal of Women's History* 9, no. 2 (Summer 1997): 31–55.

New York City Economic Development Corporation (NYCEDC). "Raising a Glass to the Brooklyn Army Terminal's Past." June 20, 2018.

Norris, Charles. "Your Essay in Extermination." *New American Review* 226, no. 6 (December 1928): 645–52.

Nugent, Richard Bruce. "On 'Gloria Swanson' (Real Name: Mr. Wilson)." In *Gay Rebel of the Harlem Renaissance: Selections from the Work of Richard Bruce Nugent*, edited by Thomas H. Wirth. Durham, NC: Duke University Press, 2002.

NY Facts You Ought to Know. "The Bronx." nyfacts.com.

NYFood Museum. "Beer." nyfoodmuseum.org/bkbeer.htm.

O'Hara, John. *Appointment in Semara*. New York: Vintage, 2003.

Okrent, Daniel. *Last Call: The Rise and Fall of Prohibition*. New York: Simon & Schuster, 2010.

Old Timer, The. "How Prohibition Changed Ridgewood and Glendale Forever: Our Neighborhood, The Way It Was." QNS, qns.com. January 13, 2018.

Osofsky, Gilbert. *Harlem: The Making of a Ghetto; Negro New York, 1890–1930*. New York: Harper, 1971.

Ostandler, Gilman M. "The Revolution of Morals." In *Change and Continuity in Twentieth Century America*, edited by John Braeman, Robert Hamlett Bremner and David Brody. Columbus: Ohio State University Press, 1968.

Ottley, Roi. *New World A-Coming: Inside Black America*. Boston: Houghton Mifflin, 1943.

Peiss, Kathy. *Cheap Amusements: Working Women and Leisure in Turn-of-the-Century New York*. Philadelphia: Temple University Press, 1986.

———. *Hope in a Jar: The Making of America's Beauty Culture*. New York: Henry Holt & Company. 1998.

Peretti, Burton. *Jazz in American Culture*. Chicago: Ivan R. Dee, 1997.

———. *Nightclub City: Politics & Amusement in Manhattan*. Philadelphia: University of Pennsylvania Press, 2007.

Pollan, Michael. *The Botany of Desire: A Plant's-Eye View of the World*. New York: Random House, 2002.

Queens Historical Society. "Queens History Timeline." https://queenshistoricalsociety.org/queens-history-timeline.

Reagan, Nancy. "Just Say No." September 14, 1986. Archives of Woman's Political Communications, Iowa State University.

Regan, Gary. *The Joy of Mixology: The Consummate Guide to the Bartender's Craft*. New York: Penguin, 2018.

Reynolds, Quentin. *I, Willie Sutton*. New York: Farrar, Straus, 1953.

Riis, Jacob A. *How the Other Half Lives: Studies Among the Tenements of New York*. New York: Dover, 1971.

Robertson, Stephen, Shane White, Steven Garton and Graham White. "This Harlem Life: Black Families and Everyday Life in the 1920s and 1930s." *Journal of Social History* (Fall 2010): 97–122.

Rosen, Ruth. *The Lost Sisterhood: Prostitution in America, 1900–1918*. Baltimore: Johns Hopkins University Press, 1982.

Samuels, Wilfred D. *A Gift of Story/Encyclopedia of African-American Literature*. New York: Facts On File, 2007.

Sandke, Randall. *Where the Dark and the Light Folks Meet: Race and the Mythology, Politics, and Business of Jazz*. Lanham, MD: Scarecrow Press, 2010.

Sanford, E.P. "The Illegal Alcohol Traffic." *Annals of the American Academy of Political and Social Science* 163 (September 1932): 39–45.

Sante, Luc. *Low Life: Lures and Snares of Old New York*. New York: Vantage, 1992.

Shirley, Glenn. *Hello, Sucker: The Story of Texas Guinan*. Austin, TX: Eakin Press, 1989.

Sinclair, Andrew. *Prohibition: The Era of Excess*. Boston: Little Brown, 1962.

Smith, Willie the Lion, with George Hoefer. *Music on My Mind: The Memoirs of an American Pianist.* New York: DaCapo Press, 1975.

Stein, John S., and Hayward Grace. "Hello Sucker: The Life of Texas Guinan." Unpublished manuscript, 1941, NYPL, Lincoln Center Library.

Stencell, A.W. *Girl Show: Into the Canvas World of Bump and Grind*. Toronto: ECW Press, 1999.

Sylvester, Robert. *No Cover Charge: A Backward Look at the Night Club*. New York: Dial Press, 1956.

Teachout, Terry. *Pops: A Life of Louis Armstrong*. Boston: Houghton Mifflin Harcourt, 2009.

Thirteen/WNET. "A Walk Through Queens with David Hartman and Historian Barry Lewis." www.thirteen.org/queens/about.html

Thomas, Jerry. *The Bar-Tender's Guide or How to Mix Drinks*. N.p., 1862.

Thompson, Cole. "My Inwood." myinwood.net

Thornton, Mark. "Alcohol Prohibition Was a Failure." Cato Institute Policy Analysis. July 17, 1991. cato.org.

———. *The Economics of Prohibition*. Salt Lake City: University of Utah Press, 1991.

Thurman, Wallace. *Negro Life in New York's Harlem*. New York: Haldeman-Julius Company, 1928.

Timner, W.E. *Ellington: The Recorded Music of Duke Ellington and His Sidemen*. 3rd ed. Metuchen, NJ: Scarecrow Press, 1988.

Trachtenberg, Leo. "Texas Guinan: Queen of the Night," *City Journal*, Spring 1998.

U.S. Dept of Labor, Bureau of Labor Statistics, "CPI Inflation Calculator." www.bls.gov/data/inflation_calculator.htm.

U.S. Government. Commission on the Review of National Policy toward Gambling, 1976.

Vail, Ken. *Duke's Diary, Part One: The Life of Duke Ellington, 1927–1950*. Lanham, MD: Scarecrow Press, 2002.

Van Vechten, Carl. *Keep A-inchin' Along: Selected Writings of Carl Van Vechten about Black Art and Letters*. Bruce Kellner, ed. Westport, CT: Greenwood Press, 1979.

———. "My Friend: James Weldon Johnson." Fisk University, Department of Publicity, 1938.

———. *Nigger Heaven*. Urbana: University of Illinois, 2000.

———. *The Splendid Drunken Twenties: Selections from the Daybooks, 1920–1930*. Edited by Bruce Kellner. Urbana: University of Illinois Press, 2003.

Vogel, Shane. *The Scene of Harlem Cabaret: Race, Sexuality, Performance*. Chicago: University of Chicago Press, 2009.

Waggoner, Susan, and Robert Markel. *Cocktail Hour: Authentic Recipes and Illustrations from 1920 to 1960*. New York: Stewart, Tabori & Chang, 2006.

Walker, Stanley. *The Night Club Era*. Baltimore: Johns Hopkins University Press, 1999.

Walsh, George. *Gentleman Jimmy Walker: Mayor of the Jazz Age*. New York: Praeger, 1974.

Warburton, Clark. *The Economic Results of Prohibition*. New York: Columbia University Press, 1932.

Ware, Caroline F. *Greenwich Village, 1920–1930*. Berkeley: University of California Press, 1994.

Wasserman, Ira. "The Effects of War and Alcohol Consumption Patterns on Suicide: United States, 1910–1933." *Social Forces* 68 (1989): 513–30.

Watson, Steven. *Strange Bedfellows: The First American Avant-Guard*. New York: Abbeville Press, 1991.

Weiner, Deborah Grace. *On the Sunny Side of the Street: The Life and Lyrics of Dorothy Fields*. New York: Schirmer, 1997.

White, Claire. "World War I Played Key Role in Passage of Prohibition." *Mob Museum*, November 10, 2018.

Williams, Linda. *Hard Core: Power, Pleasure, and the "Frenzy of the Visible."* Berkeley: University of California Press, 1989.

Wilson, James F. *Bulldaggers, Pansies, and Chocolate Babies: Performance, Race, and Sexuality in the Harlem Renaissance*. Ann Arbor: University of Michigan Press, 2010.

Wilson, Philip K. "Bad Habits and Bad Genes: Early 20th-Century Eugenic Attempts to Eliminate Syphilis and Associated 'Defects' from the United States." *Canadian Bulletin of Medical History* 20, no. 1 (Spring 2003): 11–41.

Woolner, Christina Anne. "The Famous Lady Lovers: African American Women and Same-Sex Desire from Reconstruction to World War II." PhD dissertation, University of Michigan, 2014.

ABOUT THE AUTHOR

David Rosen is a writer and a media-tech business-development specialist.

He is the author of three books: *Sex, Sin & Subversion: The Transformation of 1950s New York's Forbidden into America's New Normal* (Skyhorse, 2016), nominated for the 2017 Bonnie and Vern Bullough Book Award by the Foundation for the Scientific Study of Sexuality (FSSS); *Sex Scandal America*: *Politics & The Ritual of Public Shaming* (Key Publishing, 2009); and *Off-Hollywood: The Making & Marketing of Independent Films* (Grove, 1991), originally commissioned by the Sundance Institute and the Independent Feature Project.

He has also published numerous academic studies, book reviews and popular pieces as well as chapters for nonfiction anthologies. See www.DavidRosenWrites.com for more information.

For information about his professional experience, check out www.DavidRosenConsultants.com. He can be reached at drosennyc@verizon.net.